The Art of Business Programming

The Art of Business Programming

with dBASE III PLUS and IV

Shimon Schocken
Information Systems Department
Leonard N. Stern School of Business
New York University

 Mitchell McGRAW-HILL
New York St. Louis San Francisco Auckland Bogotá Caracas Hamburg
Lisbon London Madrid Mexico Milan Montreal New Delhi Paris
San Juan São Paulo Singapore Sydney Tokyo Toronto Watsonville

To My Mother
Devora Schocken

Sponsoring editor: Stephen Mitchell
Editorial assistant: Denise Nickeson
Director of production: Jane Somers
Production assistant: Leslie Austin
Project management: Business Media Resources
Cover design: Jim Love
Text design: Business Media Resources
Printer and binder: R.R. Donnelley and Sons

Mitchell **McGraw Hill**, Watsonville, CA 95076

The Art of Business Programming with dBASE III PLUS and IV

1 2 3 4 5 6 7 8 9 0 DOC DOC 9 0 9 8 7 6 5 4 3 2

ORDER INFORMATION
ISBN   0-07-056919-3

Library of Congress Card Catalog No. 91-067525

Acknowledgments

First and foremost, I wish to thank the thousands of students and the two dozen instructors who patiently used rough drafts of the book and the software during the last three years and aided me in correcting the numerous bugs and glitches in the materials. In particular, the following NYU professors were very helpful in detecting problems and proposing solutions: Gad Ariav, Vasant Dhar, Barry Floyd, Thomas Isakowitz, Rob Kauffman, Alex Tuzhilin, and Rob Weitz. I also wish to thank my first computer science professor, Efraim Glinart of the Hebrew University of Jerusalem, whose introductory programming course took me a very long way.

Exercises 2-28, 2-29, and 2-30 were written by Professor Tuzhilin. The utility program `key-fake.com` that is included on the book's data disk was written by Charles Petzold and published by *PC Magazine*. The `drivea` program was written by Alex Bykov. If you have any comments or suggestions regarding the text or the software, please send a message to `sschocken@stern.nyu.edu`.

I hope the book and the software will serve you well, and that your students will find it interesting and enjoyable. For more information about suggested course outlines and useful teaching aids, please refer to the Instructor's Manual.

Shimon Schocken

Contents

God is in the details.

GOETHE (1749-1832)

Introduction
To the Instructor

Who Is This Book For?

This book can be used to support two types of courses: (1) required introductory courses for non-IS/CIS majors and (2) elective database management or project-oriented courses for IS/CIS majors. The book assumes the students have no previous experience with computers and no programming knowledge. Preview versions of the book have been used successfully in undergraduate, graduate, and executive-education programs in universities both in the USA and in Europe.

What Does the Book Cover?

The goal of the book is to expose the students to key *structured* programming techniques, using dBASE as a convenient, but not necessarily ideal, programming language. To that end, the book gives a *generic* coverage of such topics as data types, variables, assignments, string processing, numeric processing, input and output commands, logic, conditional branching, looping, and nesting. This material is presented in the context of day-to-day business problems in a way that resembles its use in languages like Pascal or C.

As a matter of principle, the book avoids the subjects of file processing and full-screen input/output (I/O). This is done for several

reasons. First, there are numerous books that cover these aspects of
dBASE, and there is no need to repeat this material here. Second,
most instructors have concrete ideas on how file management should be
taught in the classroom, and these ideas are probably as good as mine.
Third, the full-screen user interface of dBASE is unique compared to
other programming systems, and, given the book's focus on *fundamental*
programming, it entails a rather confusing diversion. Furthermore, this
user interface is likely to undergo dramatic changes as dBASE migrates
into environments like Windows and OS/2.

This is not to say that the instructor cannot introduce the subjects of
file management and full-screen I/O into the book. On the contrary, all
the programs that appear in the text are highly modular, and it might
be an excellent exercise to replace their line-oriented I/O commands
with full-screen **SAY/GET/READ** templates.

Toward the end of the book, the students build a reduced version of
a real system in which *variables* play the roles of fields and records. The
system is built with all the necessary hooks to file management, and the
next natural exercise would be to fill in these gaps with commands like
SEEK, **MODIFY**, **LIST**, and so on. With the exception of this particular
exercise, the book can be taught either before or after the students have
been exposed to interactive file processing or to database management.
Thus, the book provides a flexible module on structured programming
that can be easily plugged into a variety of different IS/CIS curricula.
The length of this module can be anything from four lectures to an
entire semester, depending on the course objectives and time constraints.

What Is the Book's Style?

Different instructors use different methods to teach introductory IS/
CIS material. The anecdotal approach consists of telling stories about
how people design and use information systems in the real world. The
theoretical approach concerns the methodology and theory of systems
design. The practical approach attempts to bring the students to a level
of competence that enables them to design reduced versions of real
systems. This book offers a mix of these three delivery methods, with
special emphasis on promoting analytical skills and technical literacy.
The goal of the book is not to turn the students into programmers or
systems analysts. Instead, the goal is to make them intelligent consumers
of the types of systems they will have to order, budget, and use in their
future workplaces.

The style of the book is somewhat different from that of a typical
textbook. In writing it, I was influenced by the following advice of a

master teacher: "Explaining is a difficult art. You can explain something so that your reader understands the words; and you can explain something so that the reader feels it in the marrow of his bones. To do the latter, it sometimes isn't enough to lay the evidence before the reader in a dispassionate way. You have to become an advocate, and use the tricks of the advocate's trade."[1]

Why Teach Programming?

Most introductory IS/CIS courses cover more or less the following material (not necessarily in this order): (1) hardware/software concepts, (2) programming, (3) data management, (4) spreadsheet modeling, and (5) other topics. Of these modules, *programming* is by far the most controversial and difficult subject to teach, to such an extent that some schools have decided to drop it altogether from their introductory curricula.

Indeed, the role of programming in business education always raises two pressing questions: (1) Is it desirable to expose novice students (and particularly nonmajors) to hands-on programming? and (2) Is it possible to cover programming in a meaningful way in, say, four to eight class meetings? After teaching about twenty introductory courses at NYU and at Wharton at the undergraduate, MBA, and executive-education levels, I am now convinced that the answer to both questions is yes.

First, the hands-on experience with programming promotes a host of educational benefits that cut across any academic major: it sharpens the students' analytical skills, it deepens their intellectual curiosity, and it develops their ability to think logically. The programming experience also teaches invaluable lessons about responsibility, planning, discipline, teamwork, and attention to details. Finally, it exposes the students to realistic business problems, and it gives them a set of tools that can be applied in their future jobs.

Second, I am convinced it is possible to teach IS/CIS material of almost any complexity and sophistication in an introductory course, *provided you find a simple and intriguing way to present it*. This, however, requires a tremendous investment in instructional materials. In addition to the mandatory class notes, which must be exceptionally clear, one has to develop tutorials, assignments, projects, case studies, application software, and system software. In short, it's a major undertaking, and that's precisely where this book enters the picture.

---

[1] Richard Dawkins, *The Blind Watchmaker*, Norton, 1987.

How Can I Use This Book
in Introductory Courses?

I assume you already spend about half of your introductory course on such subjects as file processing, database management, and systems analysis and design. The glue that converts these "different" topics into a cohesive business information system is programming. If you already give your students an overview of programming by using BASIC, then dBASE and this book are a natural alternative to consider. If you don't teach programming because you don't believe it can be covered in a rigorous and credible way in only a few lectures, then the book might change your mind on this subject.

Since the text and the software are highly modular, you can easily tailor them to support your individual teaching style and desired coverage. Whether you want to expose your students to a survey of conceptual programming ideas, or, rather, to a rigorous view of application development, the book offers a route to accomplish this goal. Furthermore, depending on your teaching needs, the book can be used either to supplement your class instruction, or, alternatively, to serve as a self-study vehicle. So, if you don't want to spend precious contact time on the nitty-gritty details of string processing or date arithmetic, you don't have to; the students can study this material on their own, reading the appropriate sections of the book and doing the numerous exercises as they go along. This will enable you to devote your class meetings to important topics like structured programming, file management, and systems design.

How Can I Use This Book
in Advanced Courses?

Instructors of elective IS/CIS courses (database management, systems analysis, and application development) often face the following dilemma: On the one hand, they want their students to be able to build reduced versions of real systems by integrating file processing and database management with structured programming techniques. On the other hand, many students come to these courses with little or no programming preparation.

The book is uniquely positioned to fill this void. Since it is written as a self-study, students can be expected to read it on their own, without class instruction. Indeed, experience has shown that readers with absolutely no computer experience have managed to gain considerable programming clout by reading the book and doing its exercises, without any external assistance. This is possible because in addition to the nuts and bolts of programming, the book covers many programming tricks and traps, and all the necessary details on designing, editing, debugging, and logging dBASE programs.

Why dBASE?

What software products should be used in introductory IS/CIS courses beyond the mandatory spreadsheet program? In other words, which software product is the most effective in demonstrating elementary programming, file processing, systems design, and database management concepts?

During the last decade I have experimented in the classroom with different combinations of Basic, Pascal, dBASE, Paradox, Framework, Lotus, and Quattro. At some point, I had a revelation: I discovered I wasn't interested in teaching software packages and programming languages per se. Instead, I was interested in communicating *ideas* and *principles*. Hence, I sat down and made a list of important topics I wanted to discuss in my course. Then I went back to the software zoo, looking for the product that could demonstrate this material in the most effective and least painful way. This product turned out to be dBASE, for a variety of pragmatic and pedagogical reasons:

- Most people think of dBASE as a powerful database management system with limited programming capabilities. In fact, dBASE is exactly the opposite: it's a powerful programming language with reasonable database management capabilities. Any Basic program can be rewritten in dBASE, resulting in tighter and more structured code. Hence, dBASE can be used to demonstrate programming as well as data management, within the same computational environment.

- Many courses already use a mixture of Basic and dBASE, illustrating programming and data management respectively. This is an undesirable situation, because the costs of switching from one computational environment to another in mid-course are enormous, from both a pedagogical and an administrative standpoint. Clearly, a consistent use of one paradigm throughout the course will serve to minimize confusion and simplify instruction.

- Most of the computers that our students will use in their future jobs will be loaded with some sort of a dBASE-compatible package. If they do any programming or data management beyond school, chances are it will be in dBASE. Basic is rapidly fading out as a commercial tool, and Pascal and C don't seem to catch up as user-oriented languages. dBASE is far from perfect, but it's still the de facto development environment for business applications on personal computers.

But Does dBASE Have a Future?

Well, it certainly has a rather impressive present, with thousands of installed applications and a software base that's probably worth several billion dollars. In a way, dBASE has become the Cobol of personal computers: many companies and consultants shun the idea of replacing it with another environment either because they dread the conversion and retraining trauma or because they've simply learned to live with it.

In all fairness, though, dBASE has many other virtues beyond this shotgun popularity. In spite of certain design peculiarities, it is a potent and relatively friendly environment. Given its vast capabilities, it is perhaps the only package that offers a smooth and linear learning curve, all the way from trivial file processing commands to structured programming to database management (not necessarily in this order, which is another educational virtue of dBASE). Therefore, learning dBASE skills is largely a sequential process: new commands and functions introduce themselves with little fanfare, and everything somehow fits together.

Although dBASE will certainly continue to evolve, in particular in the areas of user interface and database management, its essential programming core—commands like **IF**, **WHILE**, and **CASE**—will stay intact. This is because the programming formalism of dBASE is basically sound (in spite of some deficiencies that the book is careful to mention), and quite satisfactory for most business applications.

What Software Will the Students Have to Purchase?

The answer depends on what version of dBASE you want to use. If you wish to use dBASE III PLUS, there is no need to purchase the software. Information on obtaining the software is available from the Publisher. All the additional software which is mentioned in the text is included in the data disk provided to the instructor.

Under this setting, the students will be completely self-sufficient as far as software goes. They will be able to use dBASE and the book's software either in the school's lab or on their home computers. Once again, this will enable you to divide the book into the parts that you want to cover in class and the parts that are left to the students as homework and self-study.

If you wish to use dBASE IV, the students will have to purchase its educational version, which, unlike the educational version of dBASE III PLUS, is not free. However, please bear in mind that as far as this book is concerned, it doesn't matter which version of dBASE the students have. That is because the book uses a critical core of commands that is identical under both versions (the few exceptions are flagged in the text).

One final remark: If you are considering dBASE IV only because you have to give a brief demonstration of relational database management, please take a look at the program named **rats.prg** on the book's data disk. This program, which runs under both dBASE III PLUS and dBASE IV, is a relational interface which allows users to manipulate ***.DBF** files as tables, using relational commands like **PROJECT** and **JOIN**. If all you want to do is spend one or two lectures (and perhaps an assignment) on relational algebra, **rats** might be a free and self-explanatory alternative to **SQL**.

What's Next?

A sequel of this book, titled *The Art of Systems Design,* is presently available in a preview format (along with additional software, exercises, and transparencies). Picking up where the present book ends, the new book covers the subjects of sequential and indexed processing (both interactive and program-based), systems analysis and design, and relational database management. If you find the present book compatible with your teaching style, you may want to consider the second book as well, perhaps for other classes. For more information about obtaining a preview copy of the new book, please contact the author.

Introduction
To the Reader

If you flip through the pages of this book, you will see many examples of programs written in the dBASE language. And yet this book is not about dBASE, and actually it's not about programming either. The subject of this book is how to design computer-based information systems: systems that solve business problems, like airline-reservation systems, and systems that exploit business opportunities, like frequent-flier programs. Such systems may be constructed using a variety of alternative software tools, of which dBASE is just one example.

dBASE is used in this book for four reasons. First, it's a popular software package, especially in small- and medium-sized businesses. Second, it's an effective package, if you know how to handle it. Third, it's a mainstream package, and it lends itself nicely to demonstrating general ideas about programming, systems analysis, and data management. Finally, dBASE skills are highly marketable: even though many people can use dBASE to do some elementary data juggling, only a few people in each organization can design systems in dBASE. As it turns out, these people are in high demand.

The program of the book is as follows: Chapter 1 gives a preview of what it's like to work with a software development environment, either as an end-user or as a systems developer. It also demonstrates that in order to learn the art of systems design, one has to gain a certain degree of technical competence. This is the purpose of Chapter 2, which covers programming building blocks like numeric processing, user-interface design, and logic. Chapter 3 focuses on conditional branching, looping, and nesting—the logical architectures that form the skeletons of all computer programs. This material is then integrated with the programming building blocks described in Chapter 2, resulting in a handy collection of *generic* business programs. Chapter 4 synthesizes the book by demonstrating how a wholesome system is conceived, analyzed, and finally implemented in dBASE. The Appendix, titled "The Program Development Guide," is a technical reference section that describes the process of writing and testing dBASE programs.

Programming and systems design are similar to swimming, in the following sense: you can't learn either without first jumping into the water. In other words, you can't learn how to use a computer without using a computer. Therefore, you are expected to (1) read the text, (2) run all the examples mentioned in the text on a computer, and (3) do as many exercises as you can.

It is assumed that you have access to dBASE III PLUS, to dBASE IV, or to whatever is the present version of dBASE. It doesn't matter if it's the educational version or the real thing. Before starting to read the book, though, you must reconfigure your dBASE environment and augment it with the book's software. This simple procedure is described in the file **README**, stored on the book's data disk. Please read this file and follow the instructions required to make your dBASE environment compatible with the text.

The book is a bit condensed, and it may be useful to read it twice. I recommend doing the first reading away from the computer. Make yourself comfortable in your favorite corner, turn on some music, get the popcorn ready, and start reading. As you'll see, the book is written as though you were actually interacting with a computer. But for now, all you have to do is read the text and *pretend* you are working with a computer. You will quickly realize this is very easy to do.

It may be difficult to follow the text for more than one or two hours. After all, this is not a fascinating novel; it's just a no-nonsense book about building information systems. At some point or another, you'll probably get tired of reading, feeling an urge to *do* something. That would be a good time to consider turning on the computer. If you don't have immediate access to a computer, don't worry about it. It's probably better to let the material sink in for a day or two before you start banging on the keyboard.

The time you spend at the computer should be divided between two kinds of activity: practice and adventure, in that order. Practice consists of rereading the text and running *all* the examples on the computer. At that stage, be sure to follow the written instructions carefully, doing precisely what the book says. In the next stage—adventure—do precisely the opposite. If the book says it's not a good idea to divide a number by 0, try to divide a number by 0. If the book says you cannot use the word sum as a variable name, try the command **sum=15**. Be skeptical and curious, and remember that the worst thing that can happen is that you'll get an error message. The more errors you make, the more you'll learn.

Whether you are a beginner or an experienced programmer, you are expected to run all the examples given in the text on your computer. Kicking tires is a key element of programming, and you *must* verify that everything the book says is actually true.

Bon voyage!

How to Install the Data Disk on Your Computer

The magnetic disk that comes with the book is referred to hereafter as the "data disk." The data disk contains all the programs and files which are mentioned in the text. As you go through the chapters and do the exercises, you will be asked to modify these programs and files, and create many of your own.

As a rule, all the programs and files that you will personally create will be stored on the same data disk, building on what is already there. Now, in order to use this disk properly, you must go through a one-time installation procedure. The procedure will make slight changes to the user-interface of dBASE, making it compatible with the book's examples, and it will augment your dBASE environment with utility software that will help you develop and test dBASE programs.

Important note If you already use dBASE on your computer, the installation procedure will not compromise it in any way. It will only *add* more functionality.

The installation procedure is explicit. Instead of exposing your precious hard disk to the potential perils of an automatic batch file, we'll walk you through all the DOS commands that you have to enter in order to install the data disk on your computer. In order to do so, you have to be familiar with the following commands and concepts:

DISKCOPY, COPY, RENAME, MD, CD, subdirectory, AUTOEXEC.BAT, CONFIG.SYS, and **PATH**. If you know this material, the installation procedure will take less than five minutes to complete. If you feel that you are walking on a shaky ground, ask a friend to install the data disk for you.

It is assumed you are going to use the educational version of dBASE (III PLUS or IV—it doesn't matter). If your computer already has some sort of a dBASE system on it, the best strategy is to leave this system unaffected by your work. We will do this by installing the educational version of dBASE on a different subdirectory, leaving the other dBASE system intact.

Note that the educational version of dBASE is one hundred percent compatible with the real thing. The only difference is that the size of the data files created by the educational version is limited. At the same time, all the programs created under the educational version can be used under the real version. In short, using the educational version puts you in no disadvantage whatsoever.

The remainder of this file describes how to install the data disk on your computer. There are three installation options, and you have to choose one of them:

1. If you want to install the book software on a computer with a hard disk, and you want all the files and programs you use and create to *also* be stored on the hard disk, follow the installation procedure described in section I.

2. If you want to install the book software on a computer with a hard disk, and you want all the files and programs you use and create to be stored on a *floppy* disk (instead of the hard disk), follow the installation procedure described in section II. This option is ideal for computers in a PC lab where the hard disks are normally used in a read-only mode. This is also the recommended installation option for a networked lab.

3. If you want to install the book software on a computer with two floppy disk drives and no hard disk, follow the installation procedure described in section III.

In all three settings, the floppy disk drive can be either $3\frac{1}{2}$" or $5\frac{1}{4}$"— it doesn't matter.

I. A Hard-Disk Installation

1. If the educational version of dBASE is already installed on your hard disk, go to step 4.

2. Make a new subdirectory on your hard disk and call it **edbase**.

3. Copy all the files of the educational version of dBASE onto the subdirectory **c:\edbase**.

4. In what follows, it is assumed that the full path to the dBASE system on your computer is **c:\edbase**. If it's anything else, for example **c:\packages\dbase**, you have to replace every occurrence of **edbase** below with **packages\dbase**. (This is just an example)

5. Use **DISKCOPY** to make a copy of the data disk (*Note*: **COPY *.*** is not enough, as the disk contains subdirectories). Then store the original disk away, keeping it for a rainy day.

6. Insert the (copy of the) book data disk into drive A.

7. `COPY a:\install\*.hrd c:\edbase\*.hrd`
   `COPY a:\install\*.com c:\edbase\*.com`

8. `REN c:\edbase\dbase.exe dbase1.exe`
   `REN c:\edbase\dbase.hrd dbase.bat`
   `REN c:\edbase\config.hrd config.db`

   If the last command yielded an error message, it means you already have a **config.db** file. To replace it with the book's **config.db** file, enter the following two commands (do this only if you got an error message):

   `REN c:\edbase\config.db config.old`
   `REN c:\edbase\config.hrd config.db`

9. Make a new subdirectory and call it **c:\edbase\util**.

10. `COPY a:\install\*.prg c:\edbase\util\*.prg`

11. Make a new subdirectory and call it **c:\edbase\book**.

12. `COPY a:\*.* c:\edbase\book\*.*`

13. Make a new subdirectory and call it **c:\edbase\book\atm**.

14. `COPY a:\atm\*.* c:\edbase\book\atm\*.*`

15. Make sure that (1) your **CONFIG.SYS** file has at least **files=20** and **buffers=4**, and (2) that the subdirectory **c:\edbase** is included in the **PATH** command of your **AUTOEXEC.BAT** file. If you already have another version of dBASE installed in your computer, remove its subdirectory from the **PATH** as long as you are using the book. This will ensure that when you type **dbase** at the DOS level, the file that will get executed is **c:\edbase\dbase.bat**.

16. If the path to the educational version of dBASE in your computer is *not* **c:\edbase**, but, say, **c:\packages\dbase**, load the text file **c:\packages\dbase\config.db** into a text editor and change the line **path=c:\edbase\util** to **path=c:\packages\dbase \util** (this is just an example).

17. To run the book programs on your computer, change to the subdirectory c:\edbase\book, and invoke dBASE from there. All the files and programs you use or create will be routed automatically to this subdirectory.

18. For convenience, you may want to create a batch file called c:\edbase.bat which has two lines in it: CD c:\edbase\book, followed by dbase. This way, whenever you enter the command edbase from DOS, you'll be automatically placed in the subdirectory c:\edbase\book before dBASE is invoked.

19. If you want to use a text editor other than the standard dBASE editor, add the following line to the file c:\edbase\config.db: tedit=editor, where editor is the full path name to the editor you wish to use (e.g., C:\epsilon, C:\wp, C:\word, and so on). This way, when you enter MODI COMM prog in dBASE, the file prog.prg will be automatically loaded into your chosen editor. Whichever editor you happen to use, make sure that it reads and writes plain ASCII files.

II. A Hard-Disk/Read-Only Installation

1. If the educational version of dBASE is already installed on your hard disk, go to step 4.

2. Make a new subdirectory on your hard disk and call it edbase.

3. Copy all the files of the educational version of dBASE onto the subdirectory c:\edbase.

4. In what follows, it is assumed that the full path to the dBASE system on your computer is c:\edbase. If it's anything else, for example c:\packages\dbase, you have to replace every occurrence of edbase below with packages\dbase (this is just an example).

5. Use DISKCOPY to make a copy of the data disk (NOTE: COPY *.* is not enough, as the disk contains subdirectories). Then store the original disk away, keeping it for a rainy day.

6. Insert the (copy of the) book data disk into drive A.

7. COPY a:\install*.lab c:\edbase*.lab
    COPY a:\install*.com c:\edbase*.com

8. REN c:\edbase\dbase.exe dbase1.exe
    REN c:\edbase\dbase.lab dbase.bat
    REN c:\edbase\config.lab config.db

If the last command yielded an error message, it means you already have a `config.db` file. To replace it with the book's `config.db` file, enter the following two commands (do this only if you got an error message):

```
REN c:\edbase\config.db config.old
REN c:\edbase\config.lab config.db
```

9. Make a new subdirectory and call it `c:\edbase\util`.

10. `COPY a:\install\*.prg c:\edbase\util\*.prg`

11. Make sure that (1) your `CONFIG.SYS` file has at least `files=20` and `buffers=4`, and (2) that the subdirectory `c:\edbase` is included in the `PATH` command of your `AUTOEXEC.BAT` file. If you already have another version of dBASE installed in your computer, remove its subdirectory from the `PATH` as long as you are using the book. This will ensure that when you type **dbase** at the DOS level, the file that will get executed is `c:\edbase\dbase.bat`.

12. If the path to the educational version of dBASE in your computer is *not* `c:\edbase`, but, say, `c:\packages\dbase`, load the text file `c:\packages\dbase\config.db` into a text editor and change the line `path=c:\edbase\util` to `path=c:\packages\dbase\util` (this is just an example).

13. To run the book's programs on your computer, insert the (copy of) the data disk in drive A. Then invoke dBASE from the hard disk. All the files and programs you use or create will be routed automatically to drive A.

14. If you want to use a text editor other than the standard dBASE editor, add the following line to the file `c:\edbase\config.db`: `tedit=editor`, where **editor** is the full path name to the editor you wish to use (e.g., `C:\epsilon`, `C:\wp`, `C:\word`, and so on). This way, when you enter **MODI COMM prog** in dBASE, the file **prog.prg** will be automatically loaded into your chosen editor. Whichever editor you happen to use, make sure that it reads and writes plain ASCII files.

III.   A Two Floppy Disks/No Hard Disk Installation

1. It is assumed that you already possess a floppy-based educational version of dBASE, which is stored on one or more floppies which are either $3\frac{1}{2}$" or $5\frac{1}{4}$"—it doesn't matter.

2. Use **DISKCOPY** to make a copy of the book data disk (NOTE: **COPY**
    . is not enough, as the disk contains subdirectories). Then store
    the original disk away, keeping it for a rainy day.

3. Insert the disk from which you invoke dBASE into drive A, and the
    (copy of the) book data disk into drive B. If the dBASE disk is
    write-protected, remove the protection.

4. **COPY b:\install*.flp a:*.flp**
    COPY b:\install*.com a:*.com

5. **REN a:dbase.exe a:dbase1.exe**
    REN a:dbase.flp a:dbase.bat
    REN a:config.flp a:config.db

    If the last command yielded an error message, it means you already
    have a **config.db** file. To replace it with the book's **config.db**
    file, enter the following two commands (do this only if you got an
    error message):

    REN a:config.db a:config.old
    REN a:config.flp a:config.db

6. Make a new subdirectory and call it **a:\util**.

7. **COPY b:\install*.prg a:util*.prg**

8. Make sure that the **CONFIG.SYS** file in your DOS disk has at least
    files=20 and **buffers=4**. If this is not the case, load **CON-
    FIG.SYS** into a text editor and change it accordingly.

9. To run the book examples on your computer, insert the dBASE disk
    in drive A and the (copy of the) book data disk in drive B. Then
    invoke dBASE. All the files and programs that you use or create will
    be routed automatically to the data disk.

Technical Appendix

This appendix describes all the files that participate in the installation
procedure. There is no need to read it unless you are experiencing
some problems in using dBASE or the book's software.

CONFIG.DB: This file is to dBASE what **AUTOEXEC.BAT** is to DOS. We
use it to set the following switches: **SET TALK OFF**, **SET BELL
OFF**, **SET HELP OFF**, and **SET EXACT ON**. In addition, **con-
fig.db** changes the prompt of the educational version to ".", sets
the default path to the subdirectory where the book's utilities are
stored (**util**), defines the default editor (optional), and defines the
default drive (where all the files and programs will be stored).

KEY-FAKE.COM: This program is used to turn on the **INSERT** key before dBASE is invoked. It was written by Charles Petzold and published by the *PC Magazine.*

CONTR.COM: This program is used to turn off the **NUM-LOCK** and **CAPS-LOCK** keys.

DRIVEA.COM: This program locks the keyboard until the user has inserted a floppy disk in drive A.

DBASE.BAT: This batch file invokes **contr**, **key-fake**, and then the standard dbase.exe program (which was renamed **dbase1.exe**). In the PC lab setting (section II above) it also invokes the **drivea** program.

RATS.PRG: This program is a relational algebra interface to dBASE. It can be used to carry out natural **PROJECT** and **JOIN** operations from within dBASE. To use it, invoke dBASE, enter **DO rats** and then type **help**.

UTIL*.PRG: These are a few utility programs that help develop and test dBASE programs. They are described in the appendix "The Program Development Process" at the end of the book.

CHAPTER ONE

Getting Started

You are about to take a journey into the exciting world of business programming. This is going to be a hands-on tour, involving guided activities as well as self-directed adventures. No previous experience with computers is assumed, but enthusiasm and curiosity will be very helpful along the way.

Our major vehicle in this journey will be dBASE—a popular software package you may have heard about. dBASE means different things to different people. Programmers view it as a software development environment, designed to construct systems for other users. During the last decade, dBASE was used that way to construct thousands of turnkey systems that support inventory control, purchasing, shipping, billing, accounting, and practically every operational facet of running a business.

In contrast to expert programmers, most people exploit only a small number of the capabilities of dBASE. The typical PC user wants to manage a few data files, produce occasional reports, and print mailing labels. For example, a lawyer may want to use her computer to keep track of clients and appointments. If the lawyer will be willing to invest one weekend in learning some elementary dBASE commands, she will be able to design this simple application on her own. The resulting system will not be professional, but it'll do the job.

This chapter gives a preview of what it's like to use the computer as a novice, as well as an expert programmer. Along the way, you'll get acquainted with such things as interpreters, text editors, and WYSIWYG. If you don't fully understand some of these strange creatures, don't worry about it; we'll explore them in detail in later chapters. For now, sit back, enjoy the view, and get a general feeling of what this book is all about.

First Things First

Please turn on your computer and fire up dBASE. When you see the first dBASE screen, press the **ENTER** key. Now take a look at the lower left corner of the screen. Do you see a dot (.) with a flickering dash (_) right next to it? If the answer is yes, then—welcome aboard—it seems that your dBASE system is configured in line with this book. If what you see on the screen are cryptic words like "catalog" or "set-up," this means the book's software was not yet installed on your computer.

All the programs and files that appear in the text are stored on a floppy disk called hereafter the 'data disk.' To obtain a copy of this disk, contact your course instructor or the book's publisher. In addition to numerous programming examples, the data disk contains several utility programs that were especially designed to improve the touch and feel of dBASE for educational purposes. Therefore, before you start practicing the book's examples, you first have to augment your dBASE system with the book's software. The exact installation steps are described in the file **readme**, which is also part of the book's data disk. Please print this file on paper, read it, and follow its instructions. This procedure will take only a few minutes to complete, and you have to do it only once!

The Three Faces of dBASE

dBASE is a complex data management and software development environment, consisting of hundreds of different commands. Some of these commands can be used to customize the user interface of dBASE—the various screens, windows, and menus through which a person interacts with the computer. As a result, dBASE can be made to look remarkably different to different classes of users.

In general, dBASE offers three alternative modes of interaction:

- **Interactive** mode (also called **dot prompt level**)

- **Menu-driven** mode (also called **ASSIST** or **CONTROL CENTER**)

- **Program-driven** mode (sometimes called **batch**)

The choice of one interaction style over another depends on who you are and on what you want to do. **Programmers** and **system designers**—people who develop systems for other people—prefer to work in interactive mode, which gives them full control over the entire functionality of dBASE. **Casual users**—nonprogrammer types who use dBASE primarily for data management—typically work in menu-driven mode. **End-users**—people who use "canned" systems developed by other people—

don't have to know any dBASE at all. They interact with a custom-made user interface that shortcuts the standard dBASE commands, replacing them with readable screens they can easily understand.

The following three sections survey the main features of these three modes of interaction, demonstrating their use in the context of several business applications.

A Glimpse of Interactive Mode

Some programming languages, like Pascal and Cobol, are noninteractive. They are incapable of processing individual commands or conversing with the user in real time. Hence, in order to get anything done in these languages, one has to go through the grueling process of writing a computer program. Other languages, like Lisp, Basic, and dBASE, may be used in interactive mode: They engage the user in a **dialog**, in which the user enters a command, the system executes the command, the user enters the next command, and so forth.

The dialog with dBASE begins when you turn on the computer and invoke the dBASE program. The first thing the program will do (if you've installed the book's software) is display a dot at the lower-left corner of the screen. Through this dot (called a **prompt**) dBASE conveys to you the following message: "Dear user: I am sitting here patiently, waiting to see what you want to do next. I have all the time in the world. When you make up your mind, please type something and press the **ENTER** key. Just to show you that I am alive, I am going to keep this cursor blinking."

At some point, the user will enter a command, which dBASE will then execute. Next, dBASE will display another prompt, and the user will enter another command. This cyclical dialog will continue until the user has entered the command **QUIT**, at which point dBASE will shut itself down, putting the user back at the operating system level. To illustrate, consider the following interactive session, in which the user experiments with some elementary dBASE commands:

. `x=3`

. `y=5`

. `? x+y`

          8

. `? x-y`

        -2

```
.  ? y*6

        30
.  x+3

   *** Unrecognized command verb.
.  ? x+3

         6
```

You will see many more such **transcripts** (printed logs of interactive sessions) in this book. As a notational convention used throughout the book, the shaded part of the transcript marks the user's input; everything else in the session is generated by dBASE.

Let's try to decipher this transcript. At the beginning of the session, the only thing visible on the computer's screen was the first dot prompt. Next, the user entered the command **x=3**. This command caused dBASE to go to the computer's memory, find an empty space, stick the label **x** on it, and put the number **3** in it. This command had no output associated with it. Therefore, the only feedback the user got was the next dot prompt. The command **y=5** was executed in a similar fashion.

The next command, **? x+y**, is actually two commands in one: **+** and **?**. Accordingly, it caused dBASE to do two different things. First, dBASE added the two numbers that were previously stored in the memory locations labeled **x** and **y**. The result of this computation—the number 8— was then "passed on" to the display command, which in dBASE happens to be the character **?**. Hence, the command was eventually reduced to **? 8**. This command caused dBASE to display the number **8** on the screen. The commands **? x-y** and **? y*6** were executed in a similar fashion. As you may have guessed, the character ***** means *multiply* or *times* in dBASE.

The next command in the session, **x+3**, doesn't make sense according to the rules of the game of dBASE. If the user's intention was to check the value of **x** plus 3, he or she should have entered **? x+3**. As you see, dBASE is quite picky when it comes to violating its grammatical rules, or **syntax conventions**. In this case, the erroneous command caused dBASE to spit out a cryptic error message. The specific contents of this message are not important, but their spirit is something like this: "Dear user: I have no idea what you are trying to do. Please give it another try."

In this book, when we say "dBASE," we refer to the dBASE **interpreter**. The dBASE interpreter is a complex computer program whose *input* is either a single dBASE command (in interactive mode) or a dBASE program (in program mode). The *output* of the interpreter is whatever this command (or program) is supposed to produce. dBASE programs will be discussed and demonstrated in the next section.

Making Errors in Interactive Mode   When it comes to working in interactive mode, making errors is normal business, and you shouldn't be concerned about it. First, nobody keeps score. Second, it's very easy to fix an erroneous command: All you have to do is retype it. Third, and most importantly, remember what Oscar Wilde had to say about making errors: "Experience is the name everyone gives to their mistakes."

INTERACTIVE NUMBER CRUNCHING

In interactive mode, dBASE can be used, among other things, as a sophisticated calculator. For starters, the interpreter provides all the arithmetic operators like addition (+), subtraction (-), multiplication (*), division (/), and exponentiation (^). But dBASE goes far beyond the standard capabilities of an ordinary calculator. For example, the interpreter gives you the tremendous freedom to create as many *variables* as necessary, and to display their values whenever the need arises.

The notion of a **variable** is a fundamental concept in computer programming, and we'll have much to say about it in the next chapter. For now, think of a variable (say, **x**) as a temporary storage place. You can create a variable and put a number in it with a single command, such as **x=3**. If you later want to change the contents of **x**, all you have to do is enter a similar command, say **x=10**.

The following case and exercise illustrate the use of variables and arithmetic operations in dBASE:

> *PRODUCTION PLANNING*   A contractor wins a bid to supply 30,000 power generators to a government agency, at $110 a piece. The contractor has to set up a new production line, which costs $200,000 (fixed cost). Each unit would cost $105 to produce (variable cost). What would be the total production cost? What would be the contractor's profit?
>
> In order to cut down labor cost, the contractor considers the possibility of assembling the generators in Mexico, where the manufacturing cost of each unit would be only $70. However, it would cost $300,000 to set up a new production facility in Mexico. What would be the total production cost and the contractor's profit if the Mexico alternative were chosen?

Exercise 1-1 Use dBASE to help the contractor decide where to set up the production facility. First, put the numbers 30000, 110, and so on, into the variables *number of units* (**n**), *unit price* (**price**), *fixed cost* (**fc**), and *variable cost* (**vc**). Then use some dBASE arithmetic to compute and display the variables named *total cost* (**tc**) and *gross profit* (**profit**). (Remember that total cost equals fixed cost, plus variable cost times the number of units. Gross profit equals unit price times the number of units, minus total cost.) Then repeat the same arithmetic with the Mexico numbers. (Hint: Your session should begin with the sequence of commands **n=30000**, **price=110**, **fc=200000**, and so on. Use the variable names mentioned in parentheses throughout your work.)

INTERACTIVE FILE MANAGEMENT

A **file** is a collection of data stored on the computer's disk. People use files to keep track of things like customers, vendors, orders, restaurants, dates, and so on. In contrast to paper files, which are bulky and unwieldy, disk files are compact and flexible. They may be easily searched and updated, and their contents may be sorted and printed in many different ways. These useful manipulations are examples of what is generally referred to as **data management** or **file management**.

The previous section introduced you to the arithmetic skills of the dBASE interpreter. Notwithstanding the importance of these capabilities, they consist of only a fraction of what the interpreter can do. In particular, dBASE is an extremely effective **data manager**. A typical situation in which data management comes in handy is illustrated in the following case:

> *INVENTORY MANAGEMENT (PART I)* Musica Classica, a Philadelphia-based mail-order house for compact disks, manages its stock of CDs by using dBASE. The inventory file, called **cds.dbf**, keeps track of the following data items, or **fields**: **composer**, **title**, **orchestra**, **conductor**, **price**, **bin**, and **qty**. The last two fields record the warehouse location and the on-hand quantity of each CD title, respectively.

An excerpt of the inventory file of Musica Classica is stored on your disk, under the name **cds**. The following session illustrates how this file can be manipulated in interactive mode. As usual, the user's input is shaded. Everything else is generated by dBASE.

```
. USE cds
. LIST
```

#	COMPOSER	TITLE	ORCHESTRA	CONDUCTOR	PRICE	BIN	QTY
1	Beethoven	8th Sym.	Boston	Ozawa	15.00	H4	50
2	Mozart	Magic Flute	Vienna	Bernstein	12.95	K3	23
3	Schubert	Unfinished Sym.	New York	Ozawa	10.00	H2	8
4	Mozart	Requiem	Chicago	Solti	9.95	B4	12
5	Berlioz	Romeo & Juliet	New York	Bernstein	10.50	C2	32
6	Beethoven	Leonora #3	Chicago	Mazur	8.50	D3	11
7	Dvorak	New World Sym.	Israel	Bernstein	12.50	J3	4

. LIST FOR conductor='Ozawa'

#	COMPOSER	TITLE	ORCHESTRA	CONDUCTOR	PRICE	BIN	QTY
1	Beethoven	8th Sym.	Boston	Ozawa	15.00	H4	50
3	Schubert	Unfinished Sym.	New York	Ozawa	10.00	H2	8

. LIST composer, title, price FOR price < 12

#	COMPOSER	TITLE	PRICE
3	Schubert	Unfinished Sym.	10.00
4	Mozart	Requiem	9.95
5	Berlioz	Romeo & Juliet	10.50
6	Beethoven	Leonora #3	8.50

The first command, **USE cds**, instructs the interpreter to open the **cds** file for further processing. The second command, **LIST**, displays the contents of the file on the screen. The command **LIST FOR conductor='Ozawa'** displays only the CDs conducted by Ozawa, whereas the command **LIST composer, title, price FOR price < 12** focuses on the CDs that sell for less than $12. Note that **LIST** is a very flexible command. It can be used to display all the field values of all the records (**LIST**), all the field values of some of the records (**LIST FOR a certain condition**), and some of the field values of some of the records (**LIST some fields FOR a certain condition**). **LIST** is an essential dBASE command. (You can learn more about it by typing **HELP LIST** in interactive mode.)

Note that when you actually enter dBASE commands into the computer, there is no need to capitalize key words like **LIST** and **FOR**. As far as the interpreter is concerned, the two commands **LIST FOR conductor='Ozawa'** and **list for conductor='Ozawa'** are exactly the same. However, the command **list for conductor='ozawa'** is a totally different story. Can you see why? The following exercise elaborates on this phenomenon:

Exercise 1-2   Use the **LIST** command to carry out the following tasks: (1) Show all the works of Mozart; (2) show all the titles, composers, and orchestras conducted by Bernstein; and (3) find out who wrote "Romeo & Juliet." Hint: When you enter textual values, like **'Mozart'** or **'Romeo & Juliet'**, be careful to (a) use quotation marks, as shown, and (b) use capital letters where necessary. As you will soon discover, computers are very picky, sometimes to the extent of being dumb, when it comes to distinguishing between lowercase and uppercase letters. If you instruct **LIST** to show all the works of **'mozart'**, you'll get an empty screen. Does this mean the stock has no works by Mozart? No—it simply means that as far as dBASE is concerned, **'mozart'** and **'Mozart'** are two different names.

Exercise 1-3   Reflecting on the capabilities of the **LIST** command, and using some of your imagination, indicate three ways in which computer-based data retrieval has an impact on the day-to-day operations of Musica Classica. Generalize your thoughts, and comment on the impact of computer-based data retrieval on the mail-order business in general.

A Bit of Programming

The major player in the last section was a disk file named **cds**. Files are used to store a variety of things, including—surprisingly enough—computer programs. A dBASE program is a sequence of dBASE commands stored on a disk. People create and modify programs using a **text editor**. In dBASE, the name of the program is taken to be the name of the file in which the program is stored.

Suppose you've created a dBASE program and stored it in a file named **myprog**. Suppose the program consists of the three commands **x=2**, **y=7**, and **? x+y**, in that order. If you then enter the command **DO myprog** from interactive mode, dBASE will execute the three commands in the specified order, displaying the output **9** in the process. Technically speaking, the command **DO myprog** instructs the interpreter to (a) open the file **myprog** and (b) try to execute every line in the file as though it were an interactive dBASE command. If a command contains an error, the interpreter displays an error message and halts the program's execution. If the command is error-free, the interpreter executes it as if it were a regular, interactive command. Hence, a program is basically a sequential list of commands, waiting to be executed upon request, through the **DO** command.

PROGRAM-BASED NUMBER CRUNCHING

Programs are not born in a vacuum. They are designed to solve real problems of real people, and they are quite meaningless outside this practical context. The following case describes a typical financial problem that might benefit from a programmed solution:

> *FUTURE VALUE*   Suppose you are considering putting some money into a savings account. The key factors that will determine the future value of your investment are the sum of money you wish to deposit (**d**), the annual interest rate offered by the bank (**r**), and the number of years that your money will be locked in the bank (**n**). Let's denote the **future value** of your investment—the sum you'll be able to withdraw **n** years down the road—by **fv**. According to finance textbooks and common sense, this figure can be calculated through the mathematical formula $fv = d \cdot (1 + r)^n$. (Note that r is taken to be a fraction—for example, 0.085 for an 8.5% interest rate.)

Banks offer savings programs that vary greatly in terms of durations and interest rates. One simple way to assess the relative attractiveness of these programs is to compare their respective future values. Hence, it might be useful to have a computer program that calculates the future value of a savings program, given its advertised terms. The following program is an example of a correct, and yet *bad*, implementation of this program in dBASE:

```
01   INPUT TO x
02   INPUT TO y
03   INPUT TO z
04   w=x*(1+z)^y
05   ? w
```

Lines 1-3 input three numbers from the user, through the keyboard, and store them in three variables. Line 4 computes the future value, based on the user's input. Line 5 displays the result of this computation on the screen, using the dBASE display command, **?**.

So what's wrong with this program? In a nutshell, here is a *good* solution to the same problem:

```
01  * calcfv
02  * calculates the future value of a deposit
03  * author: Shimon Schocken
04  INPUT 'How much do you want to deposit? ' TO d
05  INPUT 'For how many years? ' TO n
06  INPUT 'At what rate (as a percentage)? ' TO r
07  fv = d*(1+r/100)^n
08  ? 'The future value of your savings is:'
09  ? fv
10  RETURN
```

Important dBASE does not permit line numbers. Therefore, the programs you write should not contain line numbers. Line numbers are used in the text for reference only.

To execute (or **run**) the program, enter **DO calcfv**. This command instructs the interpreter to execute the **calcfv** program, leading to the following program-controlled session:

```
. DO calcfv
How much do you want to deposit? 1000
For how many years? 5
At what rate (as a percentage)? 12
The future value of your savings is:
   1762.34
```

Let's see how this program works. Lines 1-3 consist of optional, and yet useful, documentation. These **comments** are optional in the sense that the dBASE interpreter ignores any line that begins with the character *****. In other words, comments (lines beginning with an asterisk) have no impact on the program's behavior. However, documentation is important because it helps people (rather than interpreters) understand computer programs, and it also helps students get better grades in programming assignments.

Line 4 is a prompt-and-input command. First, it displays on the screen the prompt **How much do you want to deposit?**, leaving the cursor blinking after the question mark. It then waits until the user has entered a number (using the keyboard) and has pressed the **ENTER** key. This number is then automatically stored in the variable **d**.

Lines 5 and 6 are similar to line 4. Line 7 calculates the value of the arithmetic expression **d * (1+r/100)^n**, the dBASE equivalent of the mathematical formula $d \cdot (1 + r/100)^n$, and stores the result in the variable **fv**.

Lines 8 and 9 display the result of this computation on the screen. The **syntax** (or general form) of dBASE's display command is a question mark, **?**, followed by an **argument**—that is, the data that must be displayed. In line 8, the argument of the **?** command is the text **'The future value of the savings is:'**. In line 9, the argument of **?** is the variable **fv**, causing the interpreter to display the current value of **fv**. This value, of course, depends on the user-supplied data—the values of the variables **d**, **r**, and **n**.

Line 10 instructs the interpreter to return to interactive mode and see what the user wants to do next.

Exercise 1-4   This exercise introduces you to the dBASE editor and to the practice of writing computer programs. Your assignment is to write and run the following program on your computer:

```
* add
INPUT 'enter a number: ' TO a
INPUT 'enter a number: ' TO b
? 'The sum of the two numbers is: '
? a+b
RETURN
```

As you see from the comment (first line), the name of this program is **add**. This should also be the name of the *file* in which the program will be stored. As a prerequisite to this assignment, you must first read the Program Development Guide (pp. 139-154) in its entirety. This will guide you through the process of writing, fixing, and testing dBASE programs.

When you have finished experimenting with the **add** program, use your printer to produce a listing of the program and a transcript that demonstrates the program's execution. If you are not sure about the meaning of phrases like "use your printer" and "produce a transcript," refer to the Program Development Guide (pp. 139-154). It's all in there.

Exercise 1-5   If you did the previous exercise, you've probably noticed that implementing a *correct* program is quite easy: You simply type it into the editor, the same way you would type a resume or a letter. Dealing with *defective* programs, though, is a totally different story.

One such program, named **calcbug**, is stored on your disk. **calcbug**—a messed up version of **calcfv**—contains several syntax errors. Your assignment is to load this program into the editor, change (edit) its erroneous commands, and test it until it produces precisely the same outputs **calcfv** produces. (Hint: The fourth line of **calcbug** contains a rather devastating bug. If you can figure it out, great. If not, delete the line and retype it. This will eliminate the bug.) Consult the Program Development Guide throughout your work.

PROGRAM-BASED DATA MANAGEMENT

Data management is a pervasive activity in every modern organization. To illustrate, let's consider the airline business. Marketing executives continuously analyze traffic data, trying to identify losing routes and price-hiking opportunities. Aircraft technicians routinely inspect and update maintenance records, determining service needs. Telephone operators continuously post thousands of reservations, day in and day out. All these people make extensive use of sophisticated data management programs, yet most of them know absolutely nothing about programming or data management, let alone dBASE. How can this be?

The explanation is that these people work with **custom-made** programs—programs that adjust dBASE to work in the styles of specific users, not the other way around. In such programs, the standard user-interface of dBASE is replaced with a program-controlled dialog, resulting in a system that converses with the user in the user's own terms. This is illustrated in the following case:

> *INVENTORY MANAGEMENT (PART II)*   Every day, several hundred people call Musica Classica's toll-free number to place orders. Many of these callers are bargain hunters. The typical exchange goes something like this:
>
> *Operator*: Good morning. How can I help you?
> *Customer*: Do you have any CDs for under $10?
> *Operator*: Let's see ....
>
> At that point the operator puts the customer on hold and starts searching the catalog (which is alphabetized) for CDs that sell under $10.

Can dBASE help here? Absolutely. Suppose the operator had access to a program, named **psearch** ("search by price"), that behaved as follows:

. DO psearch

Show CDs under what price? 12

```
#   COMPOSER    TITLE               PRICE
3   Schubert    Unfinished Sym.     10.00
4   Mozart      Requiem              9.95
5   Berlioz     Romeo & Juliet      10.50
6   Beethoven   Leonora #3           8.50
```

As usual, the operator's input is shaded. Everything else is generated by the **psearch** program. As you see, the program displayed all the CDs whose selling price is less than $12. The key thing to observe here is that **psearch** will work equally well with *any* user-supplied price, not just $12. This is illustrated in the following example:

. DO psearch

Show CDs under what price? 10

```
#   COMPOSER    TITLE       PRICE
4   Mozart      Requiem      9.95
6   Beethoven   Leonora #3   8.50
```

So **psearch** is quite a useful program. It lets the operator skim through thousands of CDs and in a just a few seconds put together a list of bargains for any specified budget. One might expect that such a program would be long and complex. In fact, it's only eight lines long, of which four are comments:

```
01 * psearch
02 * This program displays all the CDs
03 * in stock that sell for less than
04 * a user-supplied price.
05 USE cds
06 INPUT 'Show CDs under what price? ' TO p
07 LIST composer, title, price FOR price < p
08 RETURN
```

The star of this program is line 7: **LIST composer, title, price, qty FOR price < p**. We've seen earlier interactive commands like **LIST composer, title, price FOR price < 12**.

The unique thing about line 7 is that the cutoff price is not a *constant* (e.g., 12), but a *variable* (**p**). As you see, this subtle change opens up a whole world of possibilities: It enables you to design *general-purpose* data retrieval programs. The following exercise gives you an opportunity to practice this skill:

Exercise 1-6 Write a program that displays on the screen all the CDs whose on-hand quantity is greater than **x** units. Let the user determine what **x** is. For each CD, display the fields **composer**, **title**, **bin**, and **qty**. Name the program **qsearch**. (Hint: The code of **qsearch** will be very similar to that of **psearch**. You will need a different variable name, a different prompt (line 6), and a different **LIST** command (line 7). Except for these cosmetic touches, the two programs will be structurally identical.) Remember that dBASE does not permit line numbers. Therefore, your program should not contain line numbers. They are used in the text for reference only.

What about all the CDs whose on-hand quantities are between 20 and 50? What about the Mozart CDs conducted by Bernstein? What about the CDs of the Chicago Symphony Orchestra that sell for under $13? Each of these questions can be answered by a straightforward variation of the **psearch** program. It's tempting to show you these programs now, but in just a short while you'll be able to write them on your own. So stay tuned, and we'll get back to this material later.

A Taste of ASSIST

Most ordinary users of dBASE don't view it as a software development environment. Instead, they use it as a powerful data management system. The typical dBASE user wants to keep track of customers, print mailing labels to announce the opening of a new store, and list the names of all the people who don't pay their bills on time. Such things can be easily done in dBASE using 10 or so data management commands.

In order to make these elementary commands accessible to nontechnical users, the people who wrote dBASE developed a menu-driven user interface, called a **shell**, which sits on top of interactive mode. The shell allows users to invoke frequently used commands by making menu selections, instead of by typing their names at the dot prompt. In dBASE III PLUS, the shell is called **ASSIST**. In dBASE IV, it's called the **COMMAND CENTER**.

In many computers, dBASE is configured to invoke the menu-driven shell automatically. In this popular setting, when you fire up dBASE, you go straight into the shell's menus. To get out of the shell and into interactive mode, press the **ESC** key. To invoke the shell from interactive mode, type **ASSIST** (in both versions of dBASE).

Exercise 1-7   This exercise will help you get acquainted with the menus of the shell. Move the cursor around, venture into several menu selections, and remember that pressing **ESC** several times will always put you back where you came from—into interactive mode. Since the shells of dBASE III PLUS and dBASE IV are quite different, the exercise has two versions. (You have to do only one).

dBASE III PLUS USERS   Invoke the shell by entering **ASSIST**, and inspect the screen. What you see is the shell's **main menu**, with entries like **set up**, **create**, **update**, and so on. You can move from one menu entry to another by pressing the arrow keys. If you press the **F1** function key, the interpreter will display help information about the "current" menu selection. To exit the help screen, press the **ESC** key. Try it! At the end of your adventures, press **ESC** to go back to interactive mode.

dBASE IV USERS   Invoke the shell by entering **ASSIST**, and inspect the screen. There are six vertical windows, labeled **data**, **queries**, **forms**, and so on. You can move from one window to another by pressing the arrow keys. If you press the **F1** function key, the interpreter will display help information about the "current" window. To exit the help screen, press the **ESC** key. Try it! If you press the **F10** function key, a menu will pop up at the top of the screen. At that point you can either move around the menus by pressing the arrow keys or go back to the five windows by pressing **ESC**. If you press **ESC** once again, you'll return to interactive mode.

In short, the shell is a menu-driven user interface, designed to make dBASE more accessible to novice users. It's important to understand that it is no more than a cosmetic façade that sits between the user and interactive mode. As you move the cursor from one menu to another, the interpreter covertly builds the interactive command that your menu selections imply. When you finally instruct the shell to execute, the interpreter fires up the command that you've been building all along. This process will become clearer as you go through the following case and exercise:

INVENTORY MANAGEMENT (PART III)   The warehouse manager of Musica Classica is a casual dBASE user. Although she has never received any formal dBASE training, she managed to teach herself how to use **ASSIST**. In particular, she is now capable of listing the inventory file, updating its records, and printing several status reports.

Exercise 1-8   This exercise puts you in the shoes of the warehouse manager. You are required to retrieve some data from the **cds** file, using the shell. Once again, the exercise has two versions, and you have to do only one. Please note that from now on, the phrase *select x* will mean *position the cursor on top of* x *and press the* **ENTER** *key*.

dBASE III PLUS USERS   Invoke the shell by entering **ASSIST**. You will automatically be placed in the so-called **Set Up** menu. Proceed to select the **Database file** option. Then select the letter of the disk drive where the book's software is stored. Next, select the file named **cds.dbf**. When you see the question **Is the file indexed?**, answer **n**. Next, move the cursor to the **Retrieve** submenu, select **List**, and finally select the **Execute the command** option. When you see the question **Direct the output to the printer?**, answer **n**. Inspect the contents of the screen. To go back to interactive mode, press **ESC**.

dBASE IV USERS   Invoke the shell by entering **ASSIST**. Then select the **cds** file. Next, select the **use** option. (If the first option you see happens to be **close**, select it, then start all over again.) Next, select the **create** option from the **queries** window. A new screen will pop up, displaying the names of all the fields in the **cds** file. The down arrow next to each field indicates that the field will be included in the query you are specifying. To eliminate a certain field, move to that field by pressing the **TAB** key, then press the **F5** function key, which acts like an on/off selection switch (try it). After selecting and deselecting a few fields of your choice, press the "magic" key **F2** and inspect the screen. Then go back to interactive mode by pressing the **ESC** key as many times as necessary to get you there.

Before we move on to the next exercise, here's a word of caution. The standard dBASE literature offers step-by-step instructions on how to use the shell. Our approach is different. Although we will step you through critical places, we expect you to *guess* which action to take when the book doesn't give explicit directions. You might get lost once in a while, but getting lost and then seeing the light without outside help is what *learning* is all about. With that in mind, the next exercise might be a bit challenging, but give it a try anyway.

Exercise 1-9 The reorder quantity of Musica Classica is 20. In other words, when the on-hand quantity of a certain CD drops below 20 units, the warehouse manager places a new order for that CD. Use the shell and your best ability to display on the screen a list of all the CDs whose **qty** value is less than 20. (Hints: Before you **execute the command** (pressing **F2** in dBASE IV), as you've done before, you will first have to build a **search condition** in which you specify that **qty** ought to be less than 20.) (dBASE IV users: After selecting the **create** option from the **queries** window, press the function key **F10**, select the **condition** option, type the condition, then press **F2** from the condition box to execute the query.)

Anything you do in the shell can also be done in interactive mode. For example, consider the last two exercises. The answer to the first exercise in interactive mode is the two commands **USE cds**, followed by **LIST**. The answer to the second exercise is **USE cds**, followed by **LIST FOR qty<20** (try it). So what is more fun—working in the shell, or in interactive mode? Although the answer depends on the eye of the beholder, there is an economic argument for learning the latter. Since most dBASE users dread interactive mode and consider it a hostile territory, there is an opportunity here for you: Master interactive mode, and your skills will be in high demand. Master the shell, and you'll be yet another dBASE user.

Like all menu-driven interfaces, the dBASE shell is based on the notion that *what you see is what you get* (WYSIWYG). Most people think WYSIWYG is a great idea, until they realize that it also stands for *what you see is what you got.* In other words, the user's choices (and thus the system's capabilities) are restricted by the contents of the menus, which are fixed and limited. All the same, casual users can still get a lot of mileage out of the shell (especially in dBASE IV). If you need to display the customers who live in New Jersey or the suppliers who carry item #1675, or other fascinating tasks of that nature, the shell will be perfect for you.

It is therefore not surprising that many people like the shell and shun interactive mode. I often hear students exclaim, "These menus are so wonderful! You can learn them in just a few hours, and all you need to operate them is one finger!" Indeed, the shell is quite easy to use. Hence, anybody can become an expert in menu-driven data management. However, this also implies that *nobody* can become such an expert, because experts are supposed to be a scarce commodity. Therefore, instead of teaching you which finger should press which function key, we will focus on subjects that require an intellectual investment—subjects like structured programming and systems design.

To sum up this chapter, the following table lists the major characteristics of the different modes of interaction with dBASE:

Interaction Mode	Also Called	Typical User	dBASE Functionality	Required Competence
interactive	dot prompt	programmer	full	high
menu-driven	ASSIST	casual user	limited	medium
program-driven	batch	end-user	specific	low

The dBASE Industry

The granddaddy of dBASE was a data management program called Vulcan, written as a moonlighting project in 1977 by a programmer named Wayne Ratliff. In 1980 the program was sold to the Ashton-Tate company, which transformed it into a software package called dBASE II. (As a marketing gimmick, there was never a dBASE I.)

dBASE II was an instant hit. In the beginning of the 1980s there were virtually no other database management systems for personal computers. As a result, dBASE II took off like a rocket, transforming Ashton-Tate into a major software company. Then came dBASE III, dBASE III PLUS, and dBASE IV. Along the way, millions of dBASE copies were sold worldwide, and thousands of companies have automated their businesses using dBASE. In 1991, the Ashton-Tate company was sold to Borland International (another major software company) for the astounding price of $430 million. Not bad for a program that started (and still feels) like a moonlighting project!

Keeping in mind that Borland is the producer of Paradox, the historical archrival of dBASE, it remains to be seen what's in store for dBASE. Presently, dBASE and Paradox control about fifty percent and fifteen percent of the PC database market, respectively. If Borland plans to build two parallel product lines around dBASE and Paradox, then the future of dBASE is bright. If, alternatively, it intends to kill dBASE in favor of Paradox, it will fail to do so. This is because dBASE is no longer a product, but an industry. Thousands of people make their livings from dBASE consulting, programming, and training. Numerous dBASE how-to books have been published, including two in Hebrew. Billions of dollars have been invested in dBASE-based application software. In many ways, dBASE has become the Cobol of the 1990s.

In addition to the original dBASE, there are several dBASE look-alikes. The two most prominent players in this game are Foxpro (formally known as Foxbase) and Clipper. These products offer most of the functionality of dBASE, and then some. Altogether, there are about a dozen different versions of dBASE and dBASE look-alike software packages on the market. The people who sell these products are prone to hype, and with all the different names and sales pitches, a naive consumer can easily get confused.

It is therefore important to remember that in spite of certain operational differences, all these products are variations of the same theme. In particular, they all build upon a common foundation of some one hundred commands that go back to dBASE II. About one-third of these commands are trivial, consisting of setting different switches that customize the touch and feel of dBASE. Of the remaining lot, about 30 commands are essential bricks and mortar. The remaining commands are cosmetic variations of the essential commands.

The core of dBASE—the 30 essential commands—hasn't changed much during the last decade, and is unlikely to change in the future. This continuity is a side effect of the "upward compatibility" principle. In order to ensure market acceptance of new versions of existing products, software vendors must tout them as **upward compatible**. This means that anything that runs under the older version will also run under the new version. The commitment to upward compatibility means that, for better or worse, old commands never die.

In short, if you want to learn dBASE or any dBASE-related product, you need to master a critical subset of some 30 commands. Unfortunately, the dBASE literature doesn't tell you *which* of the hundreds of dBASE commands are essential or which commands are just nice to have around. This book deals with the essential commands only. Once you have gotten a grip on this basic material, the sensation of moving from one dBASE environment to another will be similar to that of moving from driving a Buick to driving a Toyota. With this analogy in mind, you should understand that this book will not teach you how to adjust the mirrors, tune the radio, or move the seats. The subject of this book is *driving*.

Additional Exercises

1-10 Consider the equation $a \cdot x + b = c$, in which a, b and c are given numbers, and x is an unknown variable. The solution of this equation is given by $x = \frac{c-b}{a}$. Use interactive mode to find the solutions of the equations $15x + 3 = 93$, $2x + 14 = 0$, and $17x + 191 = 245$. Check your answers. Did you get them right?

1-11 Suppose that your pre-tax income is $45,000 and your effective tax rate is 23 percent. Use dBASE to compute (a) your tax and (b) your net income.

1-12 This exercise refers to exercise 1-1 (page 26). Write a program, named **prod**, that (a) inputs values into the three variables **price**, **fc**, and **vc**; (b) computes the variables **tc** and **profit**; and (c) displays the values of the latter two variables on the screen. Test your program on the data given in the "production planning" case.

1-13 Find out (by trial and error) the largest number a dBASE variable can hold. (Hint: recalling that **a^b** means *raise* **a** *to the power of* **b**, the command **x=10^9** will store 1,000,000,000 in the variable **x**. In the process of doing this exercise you will probably encounter outputs like **0.1000E+40**. This notation stands for $0.1 \cdot 10^{40}$, or 1 followed by 39 zeros, which is more than the number of atoms that make up our planet.

1-14 Using the **cds** file, display the **composer**, **title**, and **orchestra** of all the works recorded by the New York Philharmonic Orchestra. (Hint: Don't forget to enclose the text **New York** in quotation marks.)

1-15 Using the **cds** file, display all the CDs that sell for any amount between $10 and $13, inclusive. (Hint: try to restrict the **LIST** command with the condition **price >= 10.AND.price <= 13**.)

1-16 Using the **cds** file, use *one* **LIST** command to display all the works composed by either Mozart or Dvorak. (Hint: instead of using **.AND.**, as you did in the previous exercise, try **.OR.**.)

1-17 Consider the following paragraph, taken from the book *Metamagical Themas* (Basic Books, 1989), in which Douglas Hofstadter describes the Lisp programming language:

> When you want to program in Lisp, you sit down at a computer and you type the word **LISP** (or words to that effect). The next thing you will see on your screen is a so-called prompt—a characteristic symbol such as a **=>**. I like to think of this prompt as a greeting spoken by a special "Lisp genie," bowing low and saying to you, "Your wish is my command, and now, what is your next wish?" The genie then waits for you to type something to it. This genie is usually referred to as the Lisp interpreter, and it will do anything you want— but you have to take great care in expressing your decision precisely.

What relevance does this paragraph have to dBASE? Explain.

1-18 Do exercise 1-2 using the shell instead of interactive mode.

1-19 Do exercises 1-14, 1-15, and 1-16 of this section, using the shell instead of interactive mode.

1-20 Based on your experience with interactive mode and with the shell, compare the pros and cons of command-driven and menu-driven user interfaces.

Building Blocks

Programming is a mix of art and engineering. It's *engineering* because it's governed by a rigid set of construction rules, and it's *art* because the same problem can be solved by many different programs. Furthermore, *correctness* is not the only criterion for judging a program's quality; simplicity, elegance, and clarity are almost as important.

In Chapter 1 you saw several examples of simple programs. In this chapter we step back and take a close look at the bricks and mortar of these programs: constants, variables, input/output operations, and logic. Be warned that this material might be a bit tedious. All the same, it provides an *essential* set of building blocks for writing dBASE programs.

Now, when it comes to dBASE, programming is what separates the women from the girls and the men from the boys. Any intelligent person can pick up a dBASE book and start manipulating files from interactive mode. But only a few people in each organization can build a *system* that supports an integrated business application, using programming. This chapter lays the foundations of that skill.

Chapter Preview

We've been talking for some time now about data management, data items, and data storage and retrieval. What is *data*, anyway? Technically speaking, the word *data* refers to a structured collection of *constants*. So what are constants? Instead of getting into formal definitions, let's take a look at a practical example:

> *ENROLLMENT STATISTICS*   The dean of a small community college is interested in analyzing the profile of the entering freshman class. He commissions a programmer to write a program that reads students' data and prints out key population statistics—for instance, the number of students coming from different regions, and the average GPA of graduates of a certain high school. The dean indicates that the only relevant data for this analysis are the students' names, ages, cities, high schools, and GPAs.

One of the students this program is supposed to process is Paul, a nineteen-year-old chemistry major from Chicago, whose GPA at Thomas Jefferson High was 3.75. Much more can be said about Paul: that he is five-feet-ten-inches tall, that he collects sea turtles, and that his favorite food is spaghetti Bolognese. All this information may be interesting, but as far as our program is concerned, Paul will be represented only through the five constants `'Paul'`, `19`, `'Chicago'`, `'Thomas Jefferson High'`, and `3.75`.

Suppose now that we want our program to process data for a few thousand students, of which Paul is just one example. This massive processing is typically done through some sort of a programmed cycle, or **loop**, which reads and processes students' data, one student at a time, until all students have been processed. One essential ingredient of this cyclical strategy is a set of "pigeon holes," or **variables**, designed to store one student's data temporarily for each individual cycle. In the present example, it will make sense to name these variables **name**, **age**, **city**, **school**, and **gpa**. The term *variable* is self-explanatory. That is, the contents of each pigeon hole changes, or *varies*, from one student to another.

One way to assign values to variables is through dBASE's **assignment** operator, =. For example, the commands **name='Paul'** and **age=19** will place the constants **Paul** and **19** in the pigeon holes labeled **name** and **age**, respectively. Alternatively, we may obtain these data directly from the user, through the commands **ACCEPT TO name**, and **INPUT TO age**, respectively.

If you feel a bit confused by this avalanche of information, that's natural. You've just walked through some of the most important building blocks of any programming language: data types, constants, variables, assignments, and input/output operations. We will now discuss each of these subjects in detail.

Data Types

How can we represent a complex real-life object, like a student, in a computer program? First, we'll have to restrict our attention to a small subset of relevant characteristics such as **name**, **age**, **gpa**, **city**, **state**, **birth_date**, **sat_score**, and so on. Note that these characteristics consist of different *types* of data.

dBASE distinguishes among four data types: numeric, string, date, and logical.[1] As it turns out, these four categories are sufficiently rich to capture the wide variety of data that are typically processed in business applications. The following table gives two examples of constants of each type:

Data-type	Examples
Numeric	45, −12.78
String	'IBM', 'New York'
Date	11/03/92, 04/01/54
Logical	.T., .F.

Constants

As illustrated in the table, constants come in four types: numeric, string, date, and logical. *Numeric* constants are numbers, like 19 and 3.75. *String* constants are strings of characters enclosed within single or double quotation marks—for example, **'Paul'**, and **"Thomas Jefferson High"**. *Date* constants assume the expected form of mm/dd/yy—for example, **10/11/87**. By convention, there are only two **logical** constants: **true** and **false**, denoted in dBASE as **.T.** and **.F.** respectively. Logical constants play a key role in programming, as we'll see later in this chapter.

Without a well-defined *context*, though, constants have no meaning. For example, consider the data set **'Philadelphia'**, **'Amsterdam'**, **'Flowers'**, and **'Boston'**. Can you tell what these constants mean? Probably not. The data starts to make sense only within the context of named *variables*, such as **ship**, **port**, **cargo**, and **destination**. We

---

[1] Actually, dBASE features a fifth data type, called **memo**. It is not an essential data type, and therefore it will not be discussed here.

see that well-named variables give meaning and structure to an otherwise anonymous and cryptic data set.

Variables

A *variable* is a chunk of main memory (one or more consecutive bytes), that has a *name*, a *value*, and a *type*. Variables are created and named by programmers whenever the need arises. A valid variable name is a string of at least one and at most ten characters that (a) begins with a letter, (b) includes only letters, numbers, and the underline (_) character, and (c) is not one of dBASE's key words like **DO**, **ACCEPT**, **USE**, and so on. Some examples of good variable names are **x**, **y2**, **qtr4_sales**, and **netincome**. Some examples of bad ones are **2y**, **qtr4.sales**, **net income**, and **list**. The last variable name is bad because **LIST** is a dBASE key word.

As long as you obey the rules for naming dBASE variables, the interpreter doesn't care which names you actually use. For example, if you want to create a variable that stores **age** data, and you decide to name this variable **uktwrewwzv**, that's perfectly O.K. as far as the interpreter is concerned. When it comes to naming variables, the interpreter assumes you take the following position: "When I use a word, Humpty Dumpty said, in rather a scornful tone, it means just what I *choose* it to mean—neither more, nor less." (Lewis Carroll).

Humpty Dumpty notwithstanding, you should always choose *meaningful* variable names—in other words, names that hint at which data the variables contain. Cryptic variable names lead to unreadable programs, and unreadable programs are difficult to maintain and extend. The following is a case in point:

> *TAKING STOCK* At the end of each month, a large New York bookstore takes stock of its inventory. All the copies of each book are counted, and the difference between this figure and the actuary inventory is written off as lost goods. The actuary inventory is computed as follows. First, the number of books that were *purchased* during the month is added to that month's *beginning inventory*. Next, the number of books that were *sold* during the month is subtracted. The resulting figure—the actuary inventory—describes how many books *ought* to be on the shelf.
>
> Mark, a junior programmer, is writing a program that implements this procedure. He decides to name his variables as fol-

lows: beginning inventory (**x**), ending inventory (**y**), purchased books (**u**), sold books (**s**), physical count (**a**), and lost goods (**g**). The program processes several inventory and accounting files, producing a neat report that gives the ending and lost inventory for every book in the bookstore. The program consists of some 70 lines of code, two of which are **y=x+u-s** and **g=a-y**.

What's wrong with Mark's program? The problem is that even though the program is mathematically correct, he will be the only person in the world who understands it. Of course, he can unveil some of the mystery by adding comments that say **y** stands for *ending inventory*, and so on. But why go through all this trouble? Wouldn't it be far better to work with commands like **inventory=beg_inv+purchase-sales**, rather than **y=x+u-s**?

There is an important lesson here: A correct program is not necessarily a good program. In fact, you would probably find it easier to deal with an incorrect but readable program that you could fix, than with a correct program whose obscure code you didn't understand. Readable programs are based on clear logic and well-named variables. Therefore, you should always take special care to create meaningful (i.e., descriptive) variable names.

NUMERIC VARIABLES

Numeric variables hold numeric constants, like 15, −19.5, and 3.1429. To illustrate one use of numeric variables, consider a payroll program that does some tax calculations. At the beginning of this program we can create a numeric variable, say **taxrate**, and give it the value 0.28 by using the command **taxrate=0.28**. We can then use the variable **taxrate** in dozens of different formulas throughout the program—for example, **tax=taxrate*income** or **net=(1-taxrate)*income**.

But wait a minute. Wouldn't the expressions **tax=0.28*income** and **net=0.72*income** do exactly the same trick? The answer is yes, as long as the government cooperates. When the government decides to boot the tax rate to, say, 31%, this program will become obsolete. In the previous setting, though, all we'll have to do is modify *one* command— **taxrate=0.31**—at the beginning of the program. This single change will automatically affect all the formulas in which **taxrate** participates, eliminating the tedium of going through the entire program and changing every occurrence of the constant 0.28 to 0.31. Of course, some U.S. Presidents insist that the prevailing tax rate is constant, not variable, but experienced programmers know better than that.

STRING VARIABLES

String variables (also called *text* or *character variables*) contain strings of one or more characters, enclosed in matching single or double quotation marks, like `'b'`, `"Lisa"`, or `'Washington Square'`. By *characters* I refer to all the symbols that your keyboard can generate—letters, numbers, and things like `&`, `%`, `#` and `+`.

Anything enclosed within single or double quotation marks is considered a string constant, including digits. So `'150.25'` is a *string* constant, consisting of six characters, whereas `150.25` is a *numeric* constant. This difference looks minor, but don't let your eyes deceive you: `'150.25'` and `150.25` are distinctively different creatures. This is illustrated quite clearly in the following transcript:

```
. x=150.25
. y='150.25'
. ? x
150.25
. ? y
150.25
. ? x*2
300.5
. ? y*2
Invalid operator.
```

In dBASE IV, instead of "invalid operator," the error message will be "data-type mismatch," which makes more sense under the circumstances. At any rate, in spite of their external similarity, the two variables **x** and **y** are inherently different. **x** is of type *numeric*, so dBASE will happily multiply it by 2, whereas **y*2** will yield an error, because dBASE cannot do arithmetic on strings.

DATE VARIABLES

Date variables store dates, like 04/01/1954 or 12/2/91. To illustrate the use of date variables, consider a program that produces an elaborate financial statement in which a certain important date (say, the beginning of a new month) must be printed in a number of different places. In such a case, it would make sense to assign this special value, say, 3/1/93, to a variable, say **date1**, by using the command **date1=CTOD ('3/1/93')**. This would enable us to use the command **? date1** to display the special date whenever the need arises.

You may have noticed the key word **CTOD** with some anxiety. This key word is necessary in order to distinguish the command **date1=CTOD ('3/1/93')** from the two naive alternatives **date2=3/1/93** and **date3='3/1/93'**. The first command will create a *numeric* variable, named **date2**, and initialize its value to 3, divided by 1, divided by 93, which happens to be 0.03—hardly the date we are interested in. The second command will create a *string* variable—**date3**—whose value will be set to the six-character string **'3/1/93'**. If *all* we want to do is *print* this date, the **date3** variable will serve us well. At the same time, we won't be able to do any *dates arithmetic* with this variable.

Dates Arithmetic   Can you tell what the date will be 173 days from to-day? In dBASE, the answer to this question can be swiftly obtained through the command **due_date=today+173**. If **today** is a date variable whose value happens to be 12/2/92, this command will correctly set **due_date** to 5/24/93.

Dates arithmetic is very useful in business applications, in which one is often required to compute all sorts of due dates, pay dates, delivery dates, and so on. Given the importance of date processing, the essential role of the **CTOD** command becomes clear: Dates arithmetic works only with variables of type *date*, and the only way to initialize a date variable in dBASE is through the **CTOD** function, as in **date1=CTOD('3/1/93')**.

In dBASE IV, the latter command can be replaced with the shorter notation **date1={3/1/93}**. In general, dBASE IV enables you to re-place the expression **CTOD(mm/dd/yy)** with the expression **{mm/dd/ yy}**, but only if **mm/dd/yy** is a constant. In other words, although **date1={3/1/93}** will work fine, **x='3/1/93'** followed by **date1={x}** will *not* work.

SYSTEM VARIABLES

Most computers are equipped with an internal battery-backed clock, ca-pable of telling today's date as well as the current time. dBASE allows access to the computer's clock through two special *read-only* variables named **DATE()** and **TIME()**. The variables are called *read-only* because although you can display their values, as in **? TIME()**, or assign them to other variables, as in **today=DATE()**, you cannot *change* their contents.

In particular, the variables **DATE()** and **TIME()** are "hooked" to the computer's clock, and their contents are automatically updated. The value of **DATE()** is updated every twenty-four hours, and the value of **TIME()** is updated every second. The details are as follows:

DATE() is a variable of type *date*. If today's date is March 17, 1991, the value of **DATE()** would be 3/17/91.

TIME() is a variable of type *string*, consisting of 8 characters. The time is recorded in military format: If the present time is 2:21:45 P.M. (2 hours, 21 minutes, and 45 seconds past noon), the value of **TIME()** would be **'14:21:45'**. Five seconds later, the value of **TIME()** would become **'14:21:50'**.

Exercise 2-1   Fire up dBASE and display the values of the **DATE()** and **TIME()** variables. Do they show the right date and time? If not, there are three potential explanations: (a) your computer doesn't have a clock; (b) the clock's battery is dead; or (c) the clock is not properly set. To reset your computer's clock, consult your operating system user's guide, or ask someone how to do it.

The Assignment Command

The previous sections gave many examples in which a value was given to a variable, as in **x=15+3**. In the programming literature, this fundamental operation is called an *assignment*. An assignment command has the following syntax: a variable name, followed by the assignment operator, **=**, followed by an expression. To illustrate, here is how the interpreter processes the assignment command **x=15+3**:

■ The interpreter determines (a) the *value* and (b) the *type* of the expression on the right-hand side of the = operator. In this case, we get (a) the constant 18 and (b) the type numeric.

■ If a variable named **x** already exists, the interpreter (a) changes its *value* to 18, and (b) changes its *type* to numeric.

■ If a variable named **x** does not exist, the interpreter (a) creates it, (b) initializes its *value* to 18, and (c) initializes its *type* to numeric.

The choice of the = character as dBASE's assignment operator was unfortunate, leading to potential confusion with the mathematical identity symbol, =. For example, consider the expression **y=y+12**. In mathematics, this equation is nonsensical: there exists no number, **y**, such that **y=y+12**. In dBASE, though, the expression **y=y+12** is taken to be a *command*, not an equation. The command instructs the interpreter to take the current contents of **y**, add 12 to it, and store the result in **y**. It is therefore recommended that you think of the symbol = in the context of an assignment command as standing for the word *becomes*. For example, the command **x=12** should read "*x* becomes 12".

Exercise 2-2 The mathematical expressions $x = y$ and $y = x$ are equivalent, yet the dBASE commands **x=y** and **y=x** are quite different. Can you explain why?

Exercise 2-3 The flip-flop problem: You are required to exchange the values of two variables, **x** and **y**. For example, suppose that **x=3** and **y=5**. Your task is to assign **y**'s value to **x** and **x**'s value to **y**, so that the subsequent commands **? x** and **? y** would display the values **5** and **3**, respectively. How would you do it?

The flip-flop problem is a simple litmus test for programming skills. If you haven't seen it before (many people have), and you can easily solve it, it may be an indication that you possess natural programming skills.

Dynamic Typing dBASE does not require that you tell it explicitly the *type* of a new variable. The interpreter will figure out the variable's type implicitly *from the type of the last value assigned to it*. For example, if you enter the commands **age=18** and **dept='Information Systems'**, the interpreter will automatically set the types of **age** and **dept** to numeric and string, respectively, regardless of their types prior to these commands.

So far, so good. Unfortunately, dynamic typing can also work against you. To illustrate, consider the possible subsequent command **age= dept**. This command is valid, but nonsensical; it seems that the programmer who entered it made an error. It would be nice if the interpreter had refused to execute this command, saying something useful like "data type mismatch." In reality, though, the command **age=dept** will get executed. Furthermore, the type of the variable **age** will be changed from numeric to string.

We must conclude that dynamic typing is actually an undesirable feature of dBASE. Life is full of uncertainties we cannot control, and we could certainly do without the added burden of never knowing the present type of a dBASE variable. A better design of the interpreter would require that variables have fixed types, and produce an error message whenever an assignment command attempts to change the type of a variable.

Input and Output

Most business programs can be broken into three relatively independent stages: input, processing, and output. In the input stage (sometimes referred to as *data entry*), the program prompts the user to enter data, which are then stored in variables. The program then goes through a processing stage in which the data are manipulated in one way or another. During the output stage, the program produces some useful information. This information is displayed on the screen, or printed on paper, or stored in a file.

Most of the commands we have seen thus far have focused on the intermediate *processing* stage. We will now discuss several commands designed to *input* and *output* data. These commands are critically important because they regulate the sensitive and error-prone process through which humans interact with computers.

dBASE has about a dozen input/output commands, like **GET**, **READ**, and **PICTURE**. These commands give the programmer full control over the computer's screen, allowing him or her to create fancy data entry and display templates. At the same time, commands like **GET** and **READ** are neither standard nor essential: they don't mean much outside the world of dBASE, and their main contribution is in aesthetics.

Therefore, for the sake of minimizing clutter, we'll restrict our attention here to four input/output commands only: **INPUT** and **ACCEPT** for data entry, and **?** and **??** for displaying results.

INPUT COMMANDS

Numeric Inputs   Numeric data are obtained through the **INPUT** command, as follows:

```
INPUT 'Enter your age:' TO age
```

The general syntax of the **INPUT** command is **INPUT prompt TO variable**. The *prompt* is an optional message that typically tells the user what kind of input is expected. The user then types something at the keyboard and presses the **ENTER** key. When dBASE senses that **ENTER** has been pressed, the user's input is automatically assigned to the *variable*.

String Inputs   Textual data are obtained through the **ACCEPT** command, as follows:

```
ACCEPT 'Enter your name:' TO name
```

The general syntax of the **ACCEPT** command is **ACCEPT prompt TO variable**. The *prompt* is an optional message that typically tells the user what kind of input is expected. The user then types something at the keyboard and presses the **ENTER** key. When dBASE senses that **ENTER** has been pressed, two things happen: (a) The user's input is automatically assigned to the *variable*, and (b) the type of the *variable* is automatically set to <u>*string*</u>, *regardless of the type of the data the user has entered.*

The last sentence is worth repeating: The **ACCEPT prompt TO variable** command always sets the type of its **variable** to string. To illustrate, consider the command **ACCEPT 'What is your annual salary?' TO salary**. Suppose the user has entered the number 35000 as a response to this command. This will cause the *string* **'35000'**, rather than the *number* **35000**, to be stored in the variable **salary**. This distinction is important because **'35000'** is not a number; it's a string of five characters that happen to be digits. Hence, a subsequent command like **tax=0.28*salary** will result in an error, because the interpreter cannot do arithmetic on strings.

OUTPUT COMMANDS

The ultimate outcome of all programs is a flickering screen or a printed page. At one point or another, all programs display something on the screen or print something on paper. Since the commands for displaying and printing data are more or less the same, we'll restrict our attention here to *displaying* only.

Specifically, we'll focus on the display commands **? expression** and **?? expression**. By *expression* we refer to numeric expressions, like **15+32/4**, and to textual expressions, like **'Los Angeles'**. The commands **?** and **??** are designed to display (or print) the values of such expressions. The details are as follows:

? expression	Skip to the next line, then display the value of the *expression*.
?	Skip to the next line, without displaying anything.
?? expression	Display the value of the *expression* in the present line.

AN ILLUSTRATIVE INPUT/OUTPUT PROGRAM

This section illustrates all the input/output commands that were discussed thus far in the context of one program. The program, named **iodemo**, serves no practical purpose; it is designed strictly for demonstration. The code of the program is as follows:

```
01 * iodemo
02 * an input/output demo
03 ACCEPT 'name:  ' TO name
04 INPUT  'age:   ' TO age
05 ACCEPT 'major: ' TO major
06 INPUT  'GPA:   ' TO gpa
07 ?
08 ? name
09 ?? ', a '
10 ?? major
11 ?? ' major, '
12 ? 'is '
13 ?? age
14 ?? ' years old.'
15 ? 'His GPA is:'
16 ?? gpa
17 RETURN
```

The following transcript demonstrates the program in action. The line numbers on the left side of each output line should help you keep track of the program's execution. They indicate which program lines were executed before that particular output line was displayed on the screen. For example, after the user has entered the command **do iodemo**, lines 1-3 got executed, causing the prompt **name:** to appear on the screen. After the user had entered **'Steve'**, line 4 got executed, and so forth.

```
            . do iodemo
1,2,3       name:  Steve
4           age:   21
5           major: Business Administration
6           GPA:   3.55
7
8,9,10,11   Steve, a Business Administration major,
12,13,14    is           21 years old.
15,16       His GPA is:          3.55
```

As you see, the output of **iodemo** is not well formatted. We will later explain how to get rid of unnecessary spaces and improve the appearance of your outputs.

Numeric Processing

Many programs involve the computation of mathematical formulas—for example $(-b+\sqrt{b^2-4ac})/(2a)$. In dBASE, such formulas are implemented through *numeric expressions* that are written slightly differently, such as `(-b+SQRT(b^2-4*a*c))/(2*a)`. The following case describes a program that carries out a useful numeric calculation.

> *TEMPERATURE CONVERSION*   In many places outside the United States, temperatures are measured in Celsius. The relationship between Fahrenheit (f) and Celsius (c) degrees is $f = \frac{9}{5} \cdot c + 32$. We wish to write a program that converts a given temperature from Celsius to Fahrenheit.

In dBASE, the mathematical formula $f = \frac{9}{5} \cdot c + 32$ is implemented by using the numeric expression `f=9/5*c+32`. The conversion program and an example of its behavior are given here:

```
01 * ctof
02 * transforms a Celsius degree (c)
03 * into a Fahrenheit degree (f)
04 INPUT 'Enter the Celsius temperature: ' to c
05 f=9/5*c+32
06 ? 'The Fahrenheit temperature is:'
07 ?? f
08 RETURN
```

```
. do ctof
Enter the Celsius temperature: 28
The Fahrenheit temperature is:        82.40
```

Again, note that the output is not well formatted. We will take care of these cosmetic details later.

Exercise 2-4   Write a program that converts a temperature from Fahrenheit to Celsius. (Hint: First, use your algebraic skills to move c to the left side of the equation $f = \frac{9}{5} \cdot c + 32$. Next, implement the conversion procedure in dBASE, using the **ctof** program as a model. Call the new program **ftoc**.)

Numeric expressions may be simple or complex. A simple expression consists of a single constant, like 197, or a single variable, like **x**. Complex expressions involve operators and parentheses, such as `(197+x)/5`, or `(-b+SQRT(b^2-4*a*c))/(2*a)`.

Let's focus on the latter expression. Note that it is made up of many building blocks: numeric constants (**2,4**), numeric variables (**a, b, c**), numeric operators (**-, ^, ***), a numeric function (**SQRT**), and round parentheses. We've already discussed numeric constants and variables earlier in the chapter. We now proceed to discuss numeric *operators* and numeric *functions*, leading to the formal definition of a *numeric expression*.

NUMERIC OPERATORS

A *numeric operator* operates on two numeric expressions, returning a single numeric value. For example, consider the expression **3 * (5 + 2)**. Here we have the operator ***** operating on the two expressions **3** and **(5+2)**. In order to complete this computation, the interpreter first applies the operator **+** to the expressions **5** and **2**, returning **7**. This value is then passed on to the previous operation, which becomes **3 * 7**. This operation finally returns the value **21**.

The following table lists the five numeric operators recognized by dBASE, along with their more familiar mathematical notations:

Math	English	dBASE
$x + y$	addition	x+y
$x - y$	subtraction	x-y
$x \cdot y$	multiplication	x*y
$\frac{x}{y}$	division	x/y
x^y	power	x^y

A numeric expression that contains several operators is evaluated in the following order: power, division, multiplication, subtraction, and addition. This priority may be altered by proper use of round parentheses (expressions within parentheses are evaluated first). The order of evaluation is illustrated in the following example:

```
6 - 5 ^ (11 - 9) / 4 + 7 =
6 - 5 ^ 2 / 4 + 7 =
6 - 25 / 4 + 7 =
6 - 6.25 + 7 =
-0.25 + 7 =
6.75
```

NUMERIC FUNCTIONS

dBASE has several built-in *numeric functions,* designed to operate on numeric expressions. For example, the function **SQRT(16)** returns the square root of 16. So if you enter **y=SQRT(16)**, **y** will be assigned the number 4, and if you further enter **z=SQRT(y)**, you can imagine what will be the value of **z**. Can you figure out what will be the value of the expression **SQRT(z^2)?**

Here is a handy selection of dBASE's built-in numeric functions, along with their more familiar mathematical notations:

Math	English	dBASE
$\sqrt{x}$	square-root	SQRT(**x**)
$\lvert x \rvert$	absolute value	ABS(**x**)
e^x	exponential	EXP(**x**)
$\lfloor x \rfloor$	integer part	INT(**x**)
$\log x$	logarithm	LOG(**x**)

NUMERIC EXPRESSIONS

Armed with all the necessary building blocks, we are now in a position to define a numeric expression formally:

A *numeric expression* is a proper combination of one or more numeric constants, numeric variables, numeric functions, numeric operators, and round parentheses, if necessary. The ultimate *value* of a numeric expression is a numeric constant.

Here are a few more examples of numeric expressions:

Math	dBASE
197	197
x	x
$x - \frac{3}{y}$	x-3/y
$\frac{x-3}{y}$	(x-3)/y
$\log \frac{1+a}{1-a}$	log((1+a)/(1-a))
$\frac{-b+\sqrt{b^2-4ac}}{2a}$	(-b+SQRT(b^2-4*a*c))/(2*a)

The interpreter evaluates a numeric expression as follows: First, expressions within parentheses are evaluated (inner expressions are evaluated first). Next, functions are evaluated. The remainder of the expression is then evaluated according to the operators' priority—power, division, multiplication, subtraction, and addition.

For example, consider the command `x=SQRT(33+ABS(-16+INT (25/3))-SQRT(25))`. This command will eventually assign the number 6 to the variable **x**, as follows:

```
x = SQRT(33 + ABS(-16+INT(25/3)) - SQRT(25)) =
    SQRT(33 + ABS(-16+INT(8.33)) - SQRT(25)) =
    SQRT(33 + ABS(-16+8) - SQRT(25)) =
    SQRT(33 + ABS(-8) - SQRT(25)) =
    SQRT(33 + 8 - SQRT(25)) =
    SQRT(33 + 8 - 5) =
    SQRT(33 + 3) =
    SQRT(36) =
    6
```

Exercise 2-5   Calculate the value of the numeric expression `2^ABS(7-12)-30/(2+INT(SQRT(2)))`

AN ILLUSTRATIVE NUMERIC PROCESSING PROGRAM

The following case, taken from the domain of operations management, illustrates a typical application of numeric processing:

> *OPERATIONS MANAGEMENT*   Suppose you are an importer of Japanese cars. Next year you expect to sell 100,000 cars in the United States. When you place a new order from your Japanese agent, you pay (a) the cars' cost, which *varies* with the order's size; and (b) a *fixed* sum of $25,000, which covers the order's processing cost *irrespective* of its size. Once you get the cars, you have to stock them in your lots, which costs you $250 per car, per year. Now here is the dilemma: In order to cut down annual shipment costs, you should place *few* (and therefore large) orders and then stock them in inventory. To cut down inventory costs, however, you should place small (and therefore *many*) orders whenever demand picks up. How many orders should you place each year?

It turns out that this important dilemma can be solved mathematically, as follows. Let the annual demand in units be *d*, the cost of placing an order c, and the annual per-unit holding cost h. According to a classical analysis that goes back to 1915, the order size that minimizes the total cost function is $q = \sqrt{(2 \cdot d \cdot c)/h}$. Since the annual demand is d, the number of orders during the year should be d/q.

The following transcript illustrates the behavior of a general-purpose program that computes the *economic order quantity*, as it is called in operations management, of any company that faces a similar dilemma:

```
. do eoq
        What is the annual demand, in units? 100000
     What is the cost of placing an order? $ 25000
What is the annual per-unit holding cost? $ 250
To minimize total cost, place an order
for           4472 units, every           16 days
```

The code of **eoq** is as follows:

```
01 * eoq
02 * finds the optimal order size
03 INPUT '        What is the annual demand, in units? ' TO d
04 INPUT '     What is the cost of placing an order? $ ' TO c
05 INPUT 'What is the annual per-unit holding cost? $ ' TO h
06 q=SQRT((2*d*c)/h)
07 norders=d/q
08 days=365/norders
09 ?
10 ? 'To minimize total cost, place an order'
11 ? 'for '
12 ?? INT(q)
13 ?? ' units, every'
14 ?? INT(days)
15 ?? ' days.'
16 RETURN
```

String Processing

All the programs we've encountered thus far have dealt with *numeric processing*. This section discusses a different family of programs—programs that manipulate *strings of characters* rather than numbers. The need for string processing programs arises in numerous situations, including the following example:

> SEARCH AND REPLACE   This book makes extensive references to the dBASE package. At the same time, the book is equally applicable to Foxpro—a dBASE-compatible package. If we wanted to develop a Foxpro edition of this book, we would begin by searching the book's text (which is stored on a disk) for strings of the form `'dBASE'`, and then we would replace each of these strings with the string `'Foxpro'`. This could be done either manually, using a text editor, or automatically, through a string processing program.

String processing is the practice of manipulating string expressions. String expressions are composed by piecing together string constants, string variables, string functions, and string operators. We have already discussed string constants and variables earlier in this chapter. We now move on to describe string *operators* and *functions*, leading to the general definition of a *string expression*.

STRING OPERATORS

The only essential string operator is the concatenation command, **+**. In general, the command **x+y** might yield three possible results, depending on the data types of **x** and **y**. If **x** and **y** are both numbers, **x+y** will return their algebraic sum. If one of them is a number and the other is a string, **x+y** will lead to an error message. If, however, **x** and **y** are both strings, **+** will act as a string concatenation operator. For example, `'U.S.'+'A.'` will return `'U.S.A.'`.

The following transcript illustrates several applications of the **+** operator:

```
. first='James'
. last='Henry'
. ? first+last
JamesHenry
 . ? last+first
HenryJames
 . ? last+' '+first
Henry James
```

STRING FUNCTIONS

dBASE offers an elaborate collection of built-in *string functions*—functions that operate on string expressions. Taken in isolation, these functions don't mean much. If you know how to put them together, though, you can make your programs sing and dance. This comes with experience.

The remainder of this section surveys a critical subset of dBASE string processing functions. It's important to read this material once, but don't try to memorize it. It should be used primarily for reference purposes.

LEN(x) returns the length of the string **x**. For example, **LEN('Information Systems')** returns the number 19. Note that *space* is also a character.

LEFT(x,n) returns the left **n** characters of **x**. For example, **LEFT ('U.S.A.',4)** returns the string **'U.S.'**.

RIGHT(x,n) returns the right **n** characters of **x**. For example, **RIGHT('U.S.A.',3)** returns the string **'.A.'**, and **RIGHT(LEFT ('U.S.A.',3),1)** returns the string **'S'**.

UPPER(x) returns the uppercase version of **x**. For example, **UPPER ('Read my lips')** returns **'READ MY LIPS'**.

LOWER(x) returns the lowercase version of **x**. For example, **LOWER ('A KINDER, GENTLER NATION')** returns **'a kinder, gentler nation'**.

TRIM(x) truncates any trailing spaces in **x**. Thus **TRIM('Ohio State ')** returns **'Ohio State'**.

LTRIM(x) truncates any leading spaces in **x**. Thus, **LTRIM(' Ohio State ')** returns **'Ohio State '**.

SPACE(n) returns a string of **n** spaces. For example, the command **x = SPACE(10)** is equivalent to (and more elegant than) the command **x='   '**.

REPLICATE(x,n) returns a string constant consisting of the string **x**, repeated **n** times. For example, the command **REPLICATE(UPPER ('a',3))** returns the string **'AAA'**. Can you rewrite **SPACE(15)** using the **REPLICATE** function?

AT(x,y) returns a number, indicating where the string **x** begins within the string **y**. For example, the command **AT('re','Where is Waldo?')** returns the number 4. If the string **x** does not occur in the string **y**, the function returns 0. For example, **AT('an', 'Los Angeles')** returns 0, whereas **AT(UPPER('an'),UPPER ('Los Angeles'))** returns 5.

DTOC(x) is a date-to-string conversion function. In order to text-process a date variable—say, **today**—you must first convert it into a string through the function **DTOC(today)**. For example, the following command extracts today's month (the two left-most characters in **today**) and stores it in a variable: **mm=LEFT(DTOC(today),2)**. To see why **DTOC** is an essential command, note that the command **mm=LEFT(today,2)** will yield an error. This is because **LEFT** can work only on string expressions.

VAL(x) is a string-to-number conversion function. **x** is assumed to be a string. For example, **VAL('599.18')** returns the number 599.18. Note: Be careful when applying the **VAL** function to nondigit strings. The function returns the value 0 in this abnormal case. For example, **VAL('gnu')** returns 0.

STR(x) is an important numeric-to-string conversion function. If the argument **x** is a numeric value—say, **3000**—**STR(3000)** returns the string **'   3000'**. Note the six spaces preceding the characters **'3000'**; if you don't specify otherwise, the output of **STR** is a ten-characters string, padded with leading spaces. If you want to be specific about the length of the output string, you can add an extra length argument. For example, **STR(3000,4)** returns the string **'3000'**, whereas **STR(3000,3)** returns an error. **STR** is also used to convert numbers with decimal places to strings. In this version, **STR** has three, rather than two, arguments, as in **STR(35.5678,5,2)**, which returns the string **'35.57'**. The first argument, **35.5678**, is the number to be converted. The second argument, **5**, is the total length of the output string, including the decimal point. The third argument, **2**, specifies how many digits after the decimal point should be retained in the output string. This fraction is rounded, if necessary.

The following transcript illustrates several applications of the **STR** function. **STR** is a commonly used tool, so these examples are worth understanding (but not memorizing).

```
. ? 3000
3000
. ? STR(3000)
      3000
. ? STR(3000,4)
3000
. ? STR(3000,6)
  3000
```

```
. ? STR(3000,3)
***
. ? STR(35.5678,5,2)
     35.57
. ? STR(35.5678,8,3)
  35.568
. ? STR(35.5678)
        36
```

Exercise 2-6 Consider the following expression: `LEFT('NewYork',1)`
`+LEFT(RIGHT('New York',4),1)+UPPER('u')`.What is the value
of this expression?

STRING EXPRESSIONS

We are now in a position to define string expressions formally:

A *string expression* is a proper combination of one or more string
constants, string variables, and string functions, that may be con-
nected by the concatenation operator, **+**. The value of a string
expression is a string constant.

AN ILLUSTRATIVE STRING
PROCESSING PROGRAM

The design of user-friendly dialogs is a key element of business programming. Most end-users are not willing to learn complicated operating
procedures, and they expect the computer to communicate with them
in their own terms. String processing plays a crucial role in achieving
such a level of communications. This is illustrated in the following case:

GRACIOUS DATA ENTRY An insurance company is testing a new
computer-based advisory system, designed to help customers get
information about different products. The system asks the customer a few questions and then suggests insurance policies and
annuities that presumably match the client's financial profile.

The advisory system is intended to serve the general public, which
includes many people with no keyboard experience. Hence, in order for
the system to be successful, it must be based on a liberal and gracious
attitude toward careless typing. The following program, named **textin**,
operates in that spirit:

```
. do textin
Good day. Please enter your name: al
How old are you, Al? 23
And where do you live? tampa
In what state? fl
OK, Al, you live in Tampa, FL, and you are 23 years old
```

As you may have guessed, effortless output requires a considerable programming effort. In order to implement a user interface that resembles English, one has to carefully piece together multiple variables and constants into complex string expressions. **Textin** is a typical example of this laborious practice:

```
01  * textin
02  * this program inputs some data of mixed types
03  * and displays them as one long string
04  ACCEPT 'Good day. Please enter your name: ' TO x
05  name=UPPER(LEFT(x,1))+RIGHT(x,LEN(x)-1)
06  INPUT 'How old are you, '+name+'? ' TO age
07  ACCEPT 'And where do you live? ' TO x
08  city=UPPER(LEFT(x,1))+RIGHT(x,LEN(x)-1)
09  ACCEPT 'In what state? ' TO state
10  state=UPPER(state)
11  sage=LTRIM(STR(age))
12  ?
13  ? 'OK, '+name+', you live in '+city+', '+state
14  ?? ', and you are '+sage+' years old'
15  RETURN
```

Textin is not a simple program; it makes extensive use of string functions, operators, and expressions. If you don't grasp it right away, that's understandable. At the same time, you *should* be able to understand this program fully once you think about it for a little while. This would require tracking the program's code and referring to the previous section on string functions.

Exercise 2-7   Answer the following five questions about the **textin** program:

1. Why is line 4 **ACCEPT**, while line 6 is **INPUT**?

2. What is the purpose of lines 5 and 8?
3. What is the purpose of line 10?
4. What is the purpose of line 11?
5. Why is line 13 **?**, whereas line 14 is **??**

Date Processing

By *date processing* we refer to the practice of inputting, manipulating, and displaying dates. The following case describes a situation in which date processing comes in handy.

> CUSTOMER SUPPORT   The New England Mariner, a Boston-based yacht builder, has a guaranteed ninety days production schedule. The customers, however, are eager to set sail, and they continually call the company to inquire about the progress of their orders. The calls are fielded by Jenny, the company's secretary. Let's assume today's date is 12/7/92. A typical exchange goes something like this:
>
> *Customer*: It's been almost three months now. Where is my yacht?
> *Jenny*: When did you place the order?
> *Customer*: 10/23/92.
> *Jenny*: Well, sir, that was only 45 days ago. As you know, our production schedule is ninety days. You should expect your yacht to be complete no later than 1/21/93. Thank you for calling the New England Mariner.

Jenny's job is not easy, but she has a secret weapon. When a customer provides an order date, she enters it into a computer program. The program—called **dates**—immediately gives her all the information she needs. This is illustrated in the following transcript.

```
. date=CTOD('12/7/92')
. do dates
Enter the order date: 10/23/92
The customer is now waiting 45 days
His expected due date is 01/21/93
```

The code of **dates** is as follows:

```
01 * dates
02 * computes the wait time and due date of an order
03 * GLOBAL VARIABLE: date: today's date
04 ACCEPT 'Enter the order date: ' TO ordered
05 ordered=CTOD(ordered)
06 days=date-ordered
07 due_date=ordered+90
08 ? 'The customer is now waiting '+LTRIM(STR(days))+' days'
09 ? 'His expected due date is '+DTOC(due_date)
10 RETURN
```

(The term *global variable* will be explained shortly.) This program demonstrates the general practice of inputting, processing, and displaying dates:

■ Input the date as a string, using the **ACCEPT** command (line 4).

■ Convert the inputted string into a date, and do whatever date processing is necessary (lines 5, 6, 7).

■ Before you display a date, convert it to a string (line 9).

DATE FUNCTIONS

The following is a useful selection of date processing functions:

DATE() is a system variable of type *date* that returns today's date. For example, if today's date were March 17, 1991, the value of **DATE()** would be 3/17/91. The value of **DATE()+30** would be 4/16/91.

CTOD(x) is a string-to-date conversion function. It converts the string **x** into a date, allowing further date processing. For example, consider the two commands **ACCEPT 'Enter your birth date' TO bdate**, followed by **x=CTOD(bdate)**. If we now enter the command **? (DATE()-x)/365**, we'll get the person's age in years. If we try the command **? (DATE()-bdate)/365**, we'll get an error message. In dBASE IV, the expression **CTOD(mm/dd/yy)** can be rewritten as **{mm/dd/yy}**, but only if **mm/dd/yy** is a constant.

DTOC(x) is a date-to-string conversion function, which is the inverse of the **CTOD** function. **DTOC** is considered a text processing function. For more information about it, refer to page 62.

CDOW(x) returns the day of the week that **x** represents, in English. For example, consider the command **x=CTOD('12/3/92')**. If we enter the command **? CDOW(x)**, we'll get the string **'Thursday'**. This tells us that 12/3/92 happens to fall on a Thursday.

CMONTH(x) returns the month that **x** represents, in English. For example, consider the command **x=CTOD('12/3/92')**. If we enter the command **? CMONTH(x)**, we'll get the string **'December'**.

TESTING PROGRAMS THAT USE DATE AND TIME VARIABLES

Obviously, a program like **dates** is date dependent: Its behavior depends on the value of the global variable **date**. The word *global* refers to a variable created and initiated *outside* the program. Why can't we use the system variable **DATE()** instead of **date**?

Recall that the system variables **DATE()** and **TIME()** are read-only; it is impossible to change their values. Therefore, we cannot test how a program that uses these variables behaves with different dates and times. To get around this problem, we can simulate **DATE()** and **TIME()** using two ordinary variables that we call **date** and **time**. The only special thing about these variables is that there is nothing special about them. Therefore, we can easily change their values in interactive mode and then observe how the program reacts to these changes. When we are confident that the program behaves well, we can get into the program's code and replace all the occurrences of the variables **date** and **time** with the real things—**DATE()** and **TIME()**.

The Role of Logic

The word *logic* means different things to different people. Common-sense logic typically refers to rational thinking. Mathematical logic is a sophisticated and fundamental branch of mathematics. Philosophical logic concerns the construction and manipulation of axioms and conjectures. When we talk about logic in the context of programming, we refer to none of these things.

In programming, the word **logic** is typically used to describe the *flow of control* of computer programs. Although a program is technically a sequential list of commands, the *order* in which these commands are executed is not necessarily sequential. Suppose, for example, that a certain program has a hundred commands, numbered 1 to 100. When we invoke the program, the interpreter might execute commands 1-12, then "branch" to execute commands 50-70, then go back to execute commands 1-12, then branch to command 73, at which point execution will be terminated. Note that some commands were executed more than once, whereas other commands were not executed at all!

The "traffic lights" that dispatch the interpreter in different directions as it executes a program are called **logical expressions**, and the *values* of these expressions determine the actual route the interpreter will take—that is, the program's flow of control. This sounds a little bit heady, so here is a simple example in which logical expressions come into play:

> *SHIPPING SCHEDULE*   When the New England Mariner has completed the construction of a yacht, it uses inland transportation to deliver the yacht to the customer. The expected delivery date is computed when the customer places the order, as follows. If the customer is located in Massachusetts or in Connecticut, and the yacht's weight is under 5000 pounds, the delivery date is set to the production completion date, plus 5 days. Otherwise, the delivery date is set to the production completion date, plus 10 days.

The delivery date is determined by a computer program that uses the following variables: **state**, **weight**, **c_date** and **d_date** (the two latter variables stand for completion date and delivery date respectively). The star of this program is an **IF** structure—something that we haven't yet seen in this book:

```
IF (state='MA'.OR. state='CT').AND.weight<5000 THEN
    d_date = c_date+5
ELSE
    d_date=c_date+10
ENDIF
```

The general syntax of the **IF** structure is:

```
IF condition THEN do something ELSE do something else.
```

The "do something" labels stand for one or more dBASE commands. The interpreter decides which action to take according to the truth value of the **condition**. If the condition is true, the interpreter pursues the **THEN** part of the program. If the condition is false, the interpreter pursues the **ELSE** part. But how can the interpreter tell whether a condition is true or false? That is what this section is all about.

All programming languages have some sort of an **IF** structure, and in all languages, the **condition** of the **IF** is implemented as a **logical expression**. Think of a logical expression as a dubious statement that may be either *true* or *false*, but nothing in between. For example, consider the simple logical expression **x>10**. If the value of the variable **x** is 11 or any number greater than 11, the value of the expression will be *true*, otherwise, it will be *false*. We see that a logical expression always has a value, and that this value must be either true or false. In dBASE, these values are denoted **.T.** and **.F.** respectively.

The following transcript demonstrates some manipulations of simple logical expressions:

```
. sales=100
. cost=50
. ? sales>cost
.T.
. ? sales=cost
.F.
. x=cost<sales
. ? x
.T.
```

The command **x=cost<sales** is interesting. It shows that the *value* of a logical expression can be assigned to a variable, in this case **x**. As you see, the type of the variable **x** is automatically set to *logical*. Logical variables are rarely used in practice, but it's good to know they exist.

Exercise 2-8   Consider the command **x=cost=sales**. Put yourself into the shoes of the interpreter, and give a detailed description in English of how you would execute this bizarre command.

LOGICAL RELATIONS

A **logical relation** makes a statement about a relationship between *two* numeric, string, or dates expressions. For example, consider **x<17**. Here, the logical relation **<** says that the value of the variable **x** (first expression) is less than the constant **17** (second expression). This assertion may be true, as in the case when **x** contains **-9**, or it may be false, as in the case when **x** contains **21**.

The following table lists all the logical relations recognized by dBASE and their more familiar mathematical notations:

Math	English	dBASE
=	equal	=
≠	not equal	<>
>	greater than	>
<	less than	<
≥	greater or equal	>=
≤	less or equal	<=

A **simple logical expression** is an *expression*, followed by a *logical relation*, followed by an *expression*. Here are a few examples of simple logical expressions:

```
12 < 15
x >= 5
city <> 'New York'
yy+12 <> 1789.12
x1*0.13 = (cost-12)/5
```

As usual, the value of a simple logical expression is either **.T.** (true) or **.F.** (false). In the example just given, the value of the first expression is **.T.**. The value of the second expression depends on the value of the variable **x**. Likewise, the values of the remaining expressions depend on the variables **city**, **yy**, **x1**, and **cost**.

LOGICAL OPERATORS

The value of a logical expression can be negated through the logical operator **NOT**. Two logical expressions can be combined using the **AND** and **OR** connectors. The truth values of the resulting expressions are determined according to the standard laws of logic, as follows:

p	.NOT. p		p	q	p .AND. q		p	q	p .OR. q
T	F		T	T	T		T	T	T
F	T		T	F	F		T	F	T
			F	T	F		F	T	T
			F	F	F		F	F	F

In these tables, the labels **p** and **q** stand for logical expressions. For example, let **p** and **q** be `city='Chicago'` and `age>35` respectively. Suppose the present values of the variables `city` and `age` are `'Philadelphia'` and `42` respectively. According to the truth tables, the value of the logical expression `city='Chicago'` `.OR.` `age>35` will be `.T.`, whereas the value of `city='Chicago'` `.AND.` `age>35` will be `.F.`. Please check it out.

Note that in dBASE the reserved words **NOT**, **AND**, and **OR** must be enclosed by periods: `.NOT.`, `.AND.`, and `.OR.`.

LOGICAL EXPRESSIONS

We are finally in a position to define a logical expression formally:

> A **logical expression** is a proper combination of one or more simple logical expressions that may be connected by the logical operators `.OR.`, `.AND.`, `.NOT.`, and round parentheses, if necessary. The ultimate value of a logical expression is either `.T.` or `.F.`.

Logical expressions are evaluated according to the following priority: (1) `.NOT.`, (2) `.AND.`, (3) `.OR.`. This default priority may be altered by the proper use of round parentheses. The process by which the interpreter evaluates logical expressions is demonstrated in the following case:

> *CREDIT LINE* A bank decides how much credit to give various customers according to several data items that are pulled from the customer's record. The decision is based on a number of rules, like the following one: *If the customer is not a student and his/her salary exceeds $30,000 or his/her net worth exceeds $100,000, then set the credit limit to $3,000. Otherwise, set it to $500.*

Before we go on, note that the bank's guidelines are confusing. In particular, the condition part of the rule can be read in three different ways, as follows:

1. If (occupation is NOT student AND salary exceeds $30,000) OR net worth exceeds $100,000 THEN ....
2. If occupation is NOT student AND (salary exceeds $30,000 OR net worth exceeds $100,000) THEN ....
3. If NOT(occupation is student AND salary exceeds $30,000 OR net worth exceeds $100,000) THEN ....

Let's assume the bank is actually referring to the second condition. With that in mind, the dBASE implementation of the rule will be as follows:

```
IF .NOT.(occupation='student') .AND.
   (salary>30000.OR.net_worth>100000) THEN
   credit=3000
ELSE
   credit=500
ENDIF
```

Suppose a certain customer has the following properties: **occupation='dancer'**, **salary=25000**, and **net_worth=70000**. How much credit will the customer get? The answer depends on the truth value of the logical expression, which is computed by the interpreter as follows:

```
(1)  .NOT.(occupation='student') .AND.
         (salary>30000 .OR. net_worth>100000)
(2)  .NOT.('dancer'='student')    .AND.
         (25000>30000   .OR. 70000>100000)
(3)  .NOT.(.F.) .AND. (.F. .OR. .F.)
(4)  .NOT.(.F.) .AND. .F.
(5)  .T. .AND. .F.
(6)  .F.
```

Hence, the poor dancer will get only a $500 line of credit.

Exercise 2-9 Consider the following dBASE commands:

```
. x=3
. y=20
. day='Monday'
. ? x<10
. ? .NOT. y<=20
. ? x>10 .OR. day<>'Sunday'
. ? x+2>5 .AND. x<100 .
. ? (y-x>20 .AND. x=y) .OR. y<22
. ?  y-x>20 .AND. (x=y .OR. y<22)
```

What would be the interpreter's response to the last six commands? Please answer using paper and pencil only. Then verify your answers on the computer.

AN ILLUSTRATIVE
LOGIC-BASED PROGRAM

It's important to realize that logical expressions are essential, and that without them there would be no programming. For example, the following problem cannot be solved without putting a logical expression to work:

> *"SMART" USER INTERFACE*   TickTech, a computer-based ticketing service, has 10,000 subscribers in the New York City area. When you log into the system, you get a welcome message that varies with the time of day. For example, if the time is 17:00 (or 5 P.M.), TickTech greets you with the message "Good afternoon! What can I do for you today?"

To demonstrate the behavior of TickTech, we'll simulate the **TIME()** variable through a global variable named **time**. The following transcript demonstrates how the program works at three different times of day (note the use of "military time," such as 17, instead of 5 P.M.):

```
. time=22          (simulating the time 10 p.m.)
. do tick

  Good evening! What can I do for you today?

. time=8           (simulating the time 8 a.m.)
. do tick

  Good morning! What can I do for you today?

. time=17          (simulating the time 5 p.m.)
. do tick

  Good afternoon! What can I do for you today?
```

The **tick** program makes use of **CASE**—a new command that we haven't discussed yet. **CASE** is a self-explanatory command, and the best way to understand it is to take the plunge:

```
01 * tick
02 * a polite "login" procedure, which gives different
03 * greetings according to the time of the day.
04 * GLOBAL VARIABLE: time (simulates system time)
```

```
05 DO CASE
06    CASE time<12
07         ? 'Good morning! '
08    CASE time>12 .AND. time<20
09         ? 'Good afternoon! '
10    CASE time>20
11         ? 'Good evening! '
12 ENDCASE
13 ?? 'What can I do for you today? '
14 RETURN
```

Exercise 2-10 The **tick** program is a good example of a readable, elegant, syntactically correct, and defective program. It contains a subtle bug related to the construction of certain logical expressions. Your task in this exercise is to (a) discover the bug, and (b) fix the program accordingly. (Hint: Think of what happens when someone logs in at noon, or at 8 P.M.)

We have used the discussion of logical expressions to introduce two new commands: **IF** and **CASE**. If you don't fully understand how these commands work, that's natural. We will have much more to say about them in the next chapter. We conclude the present chapter with two useful (but unrelated) sections on (a) how to construct fancy outputs, and (b) how to avoid bad variable names in dBASE.

Constructing Fancy Outputs

It's important to remember that the only aspect of a computer program that is visible to the user's eye is the *output* the program produces. Hence, the appearance of a program, rather than its capabilities, will often determine whether or not the program will get used in the field. Therefore, one should pay special attention to the way programs acquire data from users and display results on the screen.

Good programs produce smooth and readable output. For example, an automated teller machine might display the following message: "As of 6/11/90, your balance is $1570." This message looks and feels like an English sentence. In fact, it's a string of characters that was painstakingly crafted by a program that pieces together the values of two variables (**date** and **balance**) with two string constants (**'As of '** and **', your balance is $'**).

How can we display data of different data types in the same line, using the commands that we have learned thus far? It would be nice if we could use the following display command:

```
? 'As of ',date,' your balance is $',balance
```

Unfortunately, dBASE treats this command in an inconsistent way. Therefore, we recommend you use the following generic strategy, which you can easily adopt to any one of your programs:

1. Transform all *numeric* variables to strings by using the **STR** function. Then use **LTRIM** to trim unnecessary leading spaces. For example, transform **balance** to **LTRIM(STR(balance))**.

2. Transform all *date* variables to strings by using the **DTOC** function. For example, transform **date** to **DTOC(date)**.

3. Insert string constants like **'As of '** and **', your balance is $'**, as necessary.

4. Piece all the strings together by using the concatenation operator, **+**. This will lead to a line like **? 'As of '+DTOC(date)+', your balance is $'+LTRIM(STR(balance))**

5. If the resulting command is too wide to fit on one program line, break it into several shorter lines and use **??** as "glue." For example, the display command that was just presented is equivalent to the following three consecutive commands:

    ```
    ?  'As of '+DTOC(date)
    ?? ', your balance is $'
    ?? LTRIM(STR(balance))
    ```

6. If you wish to clear the screen (erase all the information currently displayed on the screen) before you display the next output, use the command **CLEAR**.

Exercise 2-11 The **textin** program (page 64) implements the foregoing output construction strategy. Please inspect the code of the program to be sure you understand it, with special attention to lines 11-15.

Instead of dumping the output directly to the screen, you can also accumulate it gradually into a string variable, say **line**, and then use the single command **? line** to display it in one shot. This practice is demonstrated in the following program:

```
01  * iodemo1
02  * output demonstration
03  company='Xerox'
04  date=CTOD('6/6/91')
```

```
05  price=63
06  *
07  line='On '+DTOC(date)+', '+company
08  line=line+' was trading for $'+LTRIM(STR(price))
09  line=line+' a share.'
10  CLEAR
11  ? line
12  RETURN
```

. do iodemo1

   On 06/06/91, Xerox was trading for $63 a share.

Exercise 2-12 Suppose the following commands were entered in interactive mode: **vendor='Atex'**, **price=350.95**, **order_date=ctod**
('2/5/91'), **itemno=23**, **qty=750**. Construct a string variable,
line, so that the command **? line** would display the following output on the screen (precisely): **750 units of item #23 were**
ordered on 02/05/91 from ATEX for $350.95 apiece. Test
your work on the computer (but do it on paper first).

Variable Naming Traps

dBASE III PLUS is a powerful software package, but it's not perfect.
It has several bugs and glitches that go all the way back to dBASE II.
Instead of sweeping this stuff under the rug, we'd rather put it on the
table and explain explicitly how to deal with it. A note to dBASE IV
users: Some of the problems that will be described were fixed in dBASE
IV. Please try all the examples on the computer and see for yourself.

LONG VARIABLE NAMES

The dBASE III PLUS documentation says the maximal length of a variable name is ten characters. Indeed, if you create a variable name that
is twelve characters or longer, the interpreter will display a proper error
message. There is one bizarre exception, though: The interpreter allows you to create variable names that are eleven characters long. The
eleventh character will go unrecognized by the interpreter.

    This is a subtle but dangerous bug. Most of the time, it won't affect
your work. However, on the rare occasions when it does strike, it typically
deals a brutal blow. This is illustrated in the following case:

PROCESS CONTROL Lisa, an avionics specialist, is developing a program that monitors the fuel consumption of a new airplane. The aircraft has two primary fuel tanks, each holding 1,000 gallons, and two reserve tanks, each holding 300 gallons. Lisa decides to record the tanks' capacity in the variables `fuel_tank1`, `fuel_tank2`, `fuel_tank1r`, and `fuel_tank2r`.

Lisa's programs are written in a programming language called C. Suppose, however, that she had used dBASE instead. In dBASE III PLUS, her sensible choice of variable names might lead to grave results, as the following transcript illustrates:

```
. fuel_tank1=1000
. ? fuel_tank1
    1000
. fuel_tank1r=300
. ? fuel_tank1r
    300
. ? fuel_tank1
    300
```

Do you see what is going on here? The naive programmer *thinks* she is manipulating two different variables, `fuel_tank1` and `fuel_tank1r`, yet dBASE III PLUS takes both names to refer to the same variable: `fuel_tank1`. When this blunder occurs in the context of a complex program, it might take *days* to figure out just what went wrong. And, in fact, nothing went wrong: The culprit here is the design of dBASE III PLUS, not the programmer's error. So take protective measures, and *don't even think of using eleven-character variable names in dBASE III PLUS.*

If you try to define a variable name that is *longer* than eleven characters, or a variable name that begins with a digit, dBASE III PLUS will issue error messages. The contents of these messages, however, will be quite obscure:

```
. net_income12=300
*** Unrecognized command verb.
. 1st_name='Jim'
No database is in USE. Enter file name:
```

The first error message is unhelpful, if not misleading. The second message is completely off the wall. So don't take these messages too seriously: Simply treat them as indicators that something went wrong, and feel free to ignore their contents. Also note the peculiar tone differences between the two error messages: The first begins with the alarming *******, which looks like real bad news, whereas the second message seems to be less dramatic. In reality, both errors are equally devastating, as they will end up bombing your program.

RESERVED WORDS

Almost every programming language has a list of **reserved words** that a programmer is not allowed to use as variable names. dBASE III PLUS is an exception. Of course, it has reserved words, like **INPUT**, **LIST**, **IF**, and **WHILE**, but, to the best of our knowledge, it has *no list* of reserved words. Apparently the designers of dBASE III PLUS thought such a list was not worth documenting. This may lead to some frustration on your side. For example, the variable names **sum, total**, and **count** are commonly used by non-dBASE programmers, for obvious reasons. And yet if you attempt to enter the innocuous command **sum=3** in dBASE III PLUS, the interpreter will greet you with the startling message, "No database in use. Enter filename." This is dBASE's friendly way of advising you that **sum** is a reserved word.

The solution to this problem is simple: Replace **sum** with **msum**, or something like that (using **m** as the prefix of variable names is a common programming practice in dBASE). While we are on the subject: Although **sum=3** won't work, the implicit assignment command **INPUT TO sum** *will* work, creating a variable named **sum** in the process. Also, **IF=5** will produce an error message, as one would expect, but **WHILE=12** is just fine as far as dBASE III PLUS is concerned. So dBASE is kind of fun, if you have a certain sense of humor.

Additional Exercises

2-13 Why are variables called *variables*? Why are constants called *constants*? Explain.

2-14 Suppose you wanted to represent information about *stocks* by using a set of variables, such as **company** or **price**. Which variables would you use besides these two? What names would you give them? What would be their data types? If you need some ideas, consult the New York Stock Exchange listings in your local newspaper.

2-15 Give three examples of bad variable names, and explain why they are bad.

2-16 What's the difference between the constant `-654.33` and the constant `'-654.33'`? Be specific.

2-17 Why is dates arithmetic important? Give three examples in which dates arithmetic can be used in a system that manages a doctor's office.

2-18 Compute how many days you have lived thus far. (Hint: Use `DATE()` and dates arithmetic.)

2-19 Suppose today's date is November 11, 1993. You have just promised a client you will deliver a product 75 days from now. Use dates arithmetic to determine the delivery date.

2-20 Use the `LEFT` function to display on the screen the *hours* portion of the variable `TIME()`.

2-21 Use the `RIGHT` function to display on the screen the *seconds* portion of the variable `TIME()`.

2-22 Use a combination of the `LEFT` and `RIGHT` functions to display on the screen the *minutes* portion of the variable `TIME()`.

2-23 Write a program that displays the present time in a readable format. For example, if the present value of `TIME()` is `17:33:45`, the program's output should be. **The time is 17 hours, 33 minutes, and 45 seconds.** Name the program `telltime`.

2-24 Write a program that takes an input like `'Joe Smith'` and converts it to `'Smith Joe'`. In other words, the program looks for a space character in the input, then reverses the order of the characters on both sides of the space. (Hint: You'll have to use the functions `AT`, `LEN`, `LEFT`, and `RIGHT`. Name the program `switch`, and test it on your own name.)

2-25 The area of a triangle whose sides are of lengths a, b, and c can be found through the formula $area = \sqrt{s \cdot (s-a) \cdot (s-b) \cdot (s-c)}$ in which $s = (a+b+c)/2$. Write a program that inputs the lengths of the sides of a triangle and computes its area, printing the result with two digits after the decimal points. If the user has entered the numbers—say, 7, 5, and 9—the program should print the output **triangle area: 17.41**. Test the program on the data set 7, 5, 9. Next, test it on the data set 4, 2, 8. What happened? Can you explain what's going on? Name the program **tarea**.

2-26 Suppose a savings and loans bank used the following credit rule in 1987: If the applicant is over eighteen years old or has a total debt of under $500,000, and has spent less than 15 years in jail or has a letter from a neighbor saying that he or she is a good citizen, then give the applicant a loan of $500,000. Otherwise, give the applicant only $100,000. Write down the dBASE implementation of this rule (on paper), using the variable names **age**, **debt**, **jail_years**, and **reference**. Note that the latter variable is of type *logical.* If the applicant submits a letter from a neighbor, the value of **reference** will be **.T.**; otherwise, it will be **.F.**.

2-27 Consider the following statement, made by the computer scientist Dr. Pierre DePure: "In view of the fact that the expression **.NOT.(a .OR. b)** always has the same value as the expression **(.NOT. a) .AND. (.NOT. b)**, no matter what are the values of **a** and **b**, I propose to eliminate the **.OR.** operator from all programming languages." Use the truth tables to verify that Dr. DePure's argument is correct. Then comment on his proposal.

2-28 The factorial function $n!$ stands for the product $1 \cdot 2 \cdots (n-1) \cdot n$. For example, 3! equals 6, and 5! equals 120. To shortcut this calculation, one can use the Sterling approximation

$$n! \approx \sqrt{(2\pi n)} \left(\frac{n}{e}\right)^n$$

in which $\pi = 3.14$ and $e = 2.718$. Write a program that inputs a number, n, and goes on to compute and print the value of $n!$, using the Sterling approximation. Test your program in separate runs on $n = 3, 5, 8$. Name the program **sfact**.

2-29 A system of two linear equations has two unknowns, as follows:

$$ax + by = e$$
$$cx + dy = f$$

The system has the following solution: If $ad - cb \neq 0$ then $x = (ed - bf)/(ad - cb)$ and $y = (af - ce)/(ad - cb)$. If $ad - cb = 0$ and $ed - bf = 0$ then there are infinitely many solutions. If $ad - cb = 0$ and $ed - bf \neq 0$ then there is no solution.

Write a program that inputs the numbers a, b, c, d, e, and f, and then compute and print the solution of the system implied by these numbers. Use your judgment and good taste to design the program's outputs, but be advised that it will be used by an engineer who knows absolutely nothing about dBASE. Name the program **lsystem**, and test it on the following three pairs of equations: $2x + 7y = 20$ and $5x + 4y = 23$; $3x - y = 7$ and $9x - 3y = 21$; $4x + 8y = 20$ and $x + 2y = 7$.

2-30 The Moldavian government is considering a new income tax schedule, as follows:

Gross income	Tax
<= 20000	0
> 20000 and <= 30000	15% of income *over* 20000
> 30000 and <= 40000	1500 plus 20% of income *over* 30000
> 40000	3500 plus 30% of income *over* 40000

Write a program that inputs (graciously) a person's name and gross income, and then calculates and prints the income tax based on the above table. The program would have the following user interface:

name: John Smith

gross income: 35000

John Smith, your income tax is $2500.

Name the program **inctax** and test it in separate runs on the following four people: Mike Allen ($35,000), Allen Thomas ($200,000), Thomas Michael ($10,000), and Michael Zabladowitz ($40,000).

CHAPTER THREE

Control Structures

The previous chapter described the major building blocks of *any* programming language: constants, variables, logic, and so on. We now proceed to put these different pieces together, and build about a dozen different programs that illustrate key programming ideas. Taken together, these programs amount to a handy repertoire of programming techniques that can be easily adapted to fit many different business applications.

Before we delve into some serious programming, please note that writing *real* (as opposed to *toy*) programs is unlike anything you've done before. Your programming experience is likely to be frustrating, exhilarating, time-consuming, and rewarding: "The confrontation with the programming task is so unique...that it can teach us a lot about ourselves. It should deepen our understanding of the process of design and creation, and it should give us better control over the task of organizing our thoughts." (Edgar Dijkstra)

Conditional Branching (IF)

Let's call the order by which the interpreter executes a program the *flow of control*. The programs we have discussed thus far have had a simple, sequential flow of control: all their commands were executed one after the other, in the same order in which they appeared in the code. For example, if a program, **p**, consisted of line numbers 1, 2, 3, and so on, the command **DO p** caused the interpreter to execute the commands 1, 2, 3, and so on, in that order.

83

In reality, most programs behave quite differently. They might execute a few commands and then instruct the interpreter to check whether a certain condition (which is really a *logical expression*) is true. Based on the result of this test, the flow of control might branch to different areas in the same program rather than to the next command. In *structured* programming languages, this branching mechanism is implemented through three structures: **IF**, **CASE**, and **WHILE**. The following case illustrates a problem that might benefit from an **IF** structure.

> *UNCOOPERATIVE USERS* Suppose you ask a user to enter a *positive* number and you go on to compute the square root of that number. This can be presumably implemented by the two commands **INPUT 'please enter a positive number'** **TO x** followed by **y=SQRT(x)**. It turns out, however, that this simple solution is too naive; it will not be long before a spoiler will come along and enter a negative number into **x**, precisely because he or she was asked to enter a positive number. If you don't guard against this possibility, and you proceed happily to compute the square root of a negative number, the interpreter will abort the program's execution with an error message.

This case is a typical manifestation of Murphy's Law: "Anything that *may* go wrong, *will* go wrong." When it comes to data entry, it is safest to assume the average user is as cooperative as the devil. The following program, named **csqrt**, operates in that spirit:

```
01 * csqrt
02 * calculate the square root of a number
03 PRIVATE x
04 INPUT 'Enter a positive number: ' TO x
05 IF x<0
06    ? "I can't work with negative numbers."
07 ELSE
08    y=SQRT(x)
09    ? 'The square root of '+LTRIM(STR(x))
10    ?? ' is '+LTRIM(STR(y))
11 ENDIF
12 RETURN
```

Don't worry about line 3; we'll discuss it shortly. Here are two examples of **csqrt**'s execution:

. do csqrt

Enter a positive number: 16

The square root of 16 is 4

. do csqrt

Enter a positive number: -25

I can't work with negative numbers.

The flow of control of **csqrt** begins sequentially with line numbers 3, 4, and 5. In line 5, the flow of control reaches a two-way junction; the decision of which direction to proceed in will be determined by the truth value of the logical expression **x<0**. This value, in turn, depends on the user's input, **x**, leading to the following two possibilities:

1. If the user has entered a *negative number*, the value of **x<0** will be **true**.[1] This will cause the interpreter to execute the **IF** part of the program, which in this case consists of line 6 only. The **ELSE** part of the program will be ignored. In other words, once line 6 gets executed, the interpreter will skip to the line following the **ENDIF** line, and go on to execute line 12. To sum up, if **x<0** is **true**, the flow of control will be 6, 11, and 12.

2. If the user has entered a *positive number* (or zero), the value of **x<0** will be **false**. This will cause the interpreter to execute the **ELSE** part of the program. The **IF** part of the program—line 6—will be ignored, and the flow of control will be 7, 8, 9, 10, 11, and 12. As you see, in this particular program the flow of control is completely determined by the user-supplied inputs.

In programming, the name of this behavior is *conditional branching*: upon checking a certain condition (logical expression), the flow of control *branches* to different parts of the same program. In addition to **IF**, there are two more structures in dBASE that facilitate conditional branching: **CASE** and **WHILE**. These structures will be discussed later in the chapter.

A BRIEF DIVERSION ON VARIABLE DECLARATION

In all the programs we've seen thus far, the variables were *not declared*. In other words, whenever we needed a variable, say **x**, we simply made

---

[1] Throughout this chapter, the terms **true** and **false** stand for the values **.T.** and **.F.**, respectively.

one up, as in **x=17**. It turns out that even though dBASE allows you to create variables on the fly, this is not a very good practice. In particular, when several programs and programmers work together on the same application (e.g., inventory control), one program can accidentally modify the variables of another program, leading to considerable chaos. Since good programmers use descriptive variable names like **income**, **age**, **x**, **n**, and so on, it's not surprising that the same variable names pop up in many different programs. There are two possible solutions to this problem: you can either force programmers to use unique variable names, or you can give them a mechanism to *protect* their private variables from the rest of the world. For obvious reasons, the latter solution is more desirable.

In dBASE, if you want to instruct the interpreter that a certain variable in your program, say **x**, is not the same as **x** variables in other programs (even though they have the same name), you can declare it at the beginning of your program by using the **PRIVATE x** command (see line 3 on page 84). That way, a command like **x=5** in a different program will have no effect on your own private copy of the **x** variable. Now, when we say "declare your variables at the beginning of the program," we don't mean you actually have to do it *before* you write the program. Rather, it's better that you continue to introduce new variables whenever the need arises, as we have done all along. However, before you run the program, go back to the beginning of the code and declare all its variables by using the **PRIVATE** command (thank goodness for text editors!).

THE IF SYNTAX

The **IF** structure comes in two versions:

```
IF   <logical expression>      IF   <logical expression>
     <commands1>                    <commands>
ELSE                           ENDIF
     <commands2>
ENDIF
```

In this syntax template, the **<commands>** label refers to one or more dBASE commands. The details of the two **IF** versions are as follows:

IF... ELSE... ENDIF: If the logical expression is **true**, the interpreter executes the body of commands labeled **commands1**. The interpreter then skips the entire body of commands labeled **commands2**, and goes on to execute the commands following the **ENDIF**

line. If the logical expression is **false**, the interpreter skips **commands1** and executes **commands2**. It then goes on to execute the commands following the **ENDIF** line.

IF... ENDIF: If the logical expression is **true**, the interpreter executes the body of commands labeled **commands**, and then proceeds to execute the commands following the **ENDIF** line. If the logical expression is **false**, the interpreter skips **commands** and moves on to execute the commands following the **ENDIF** line.

Warning The dBASE III PLUS interpreter is not perfect. If you forget to provide the **ENDIF** line (a very common error), the interpreter will *not* issue an error message, and will go on to execute the program as if it were syntactically correct. This will cause unexpected program behavior that is very difficult to debug.

The **IF... ELSE... ENDIF** structure was illustrated in the **csqrt** program (page 84). To illustrate the need for the simpler **IF... ENDIF** structure, consider the following case:

REGISTRATION PROCESSING A data processing company is retained to manage the registration process of a large professional conference. The basic conference fee is $250. Late registrations arriving after 7/1/93 get a $100 penalty. An optional special event adds another $50 to the total bill. When a registration form arrives at the office, a data entry operator enters the information from the form into the computer. The computer calculates the total conference fee and prints an appropriate payment remittance letter, which is sent back to the registrant.

The program that carries out this processing is called **conf_pay**. Because of the payment deadline, **conf_pay**'s behavior depends on the day on which the registration form arrives. This is illustrated in the following transcript, which tests the program on different lateness/special-event combinations (the variable **date** is used to simulate the date on which the form is fed to the program):

```
. date=ctod('6/1/93')     (test1: on-time form)
. do conf_pay
Applicant name: Paul
Special event?: n
Dear Paul, please remit the sum of $250

. date=ctod('8/1/93')     (test2: late form)
. do  conf_pay
```

```
Applicant name: Steve
Special event?: n
Dear Steve, please remit the sum of $350

. date=ctod('10/1/93')      (test3: another form)
. do conf_pay
Applicant name: Lisa
Special event?: y
Dear Lisa, please remit the sum of $400
```

```
01 * conf_pay
02 * compute the due payment for a conference
03 PRIVATE due_date,basic,event,penalty,pay,name,yn
04 * GLOBAL date (today's date)
05 * deadline and price assumptions:
06 due_date=CTOD('07/01/93')
07 basic_fee=250
08 penalty=100
09 event=50
10 * get the data:
11 ACCEPT 'Applicant name: ' TO name
12 ACCEPT 'Special event? (y/n): ' TO yn
13 pay=basic_fee
14 IF date>due_date
15    pay=pay+penalty
16 ENDIF
17 IF yn='y'
18    pay=pay+event
19 ENDIF
20 ?
21 ? 'Dear '+name+', please remit the sum of $'
22 ?? LTRIM(STR(pay))
23 RETURN
```

The logic of **conf_pay** is as follows. The program starts off with the assumption that the person owes only the basic fee (line 13). If it learns the person is late (line 14), it adds a penalty (line 15). If it learns the person wants the special event (line 17), it adds the extra cost (line 18). Finally, the program prints the invoice. Note that this logic is implemented through two consecutive and independent `IF... ENDIF` structures.

We complete the description of `conf_pay` with a few words about the `&&` characters and the global variable `date`:

In-line Comments The two characters `&&` can be used to precede an in-line comment in a dBASE program. The interpreter ignores anything between the `&&` and the end of the line.

Global Variables In order to test the ability of the program to handle deadline calculations, the programmer makes use of a global variable—`date`—which simulates the system variable `date()`. A **global variable** is a variable that is initialized *outside* the program. For more details about this testing technique, see page 67.)

THE SUBTLE DIFFERENCE BETWEEN = AND =

Consider the following two lines of the `conf_pay` program:

```
17   IF yn='y'
18      pay=pay+event
```

In these two lines, the = symbol means two totally different things. In line 17, it stands for the logical relation *equals*. In line 18, it stands for the assignment operator *becomes*.

The interpreter distinguishes between the two meanings of the = symbol according to the *context* in which the symbol appears. If the context is one of the commands `IF`, `CASE`, or `WHILE`—as in `IF yn='y'`—the interpreter infers that = is meant to be the logical relation *equals*. If the context is that of an assignment, as in `pay=pay+event`, the interpreter figures out that = stands for *becomes*. The interpreter doesn't get confused, so you shouldn't either!

Conditional Multi-Branching (CASE)

The `IF condition THEN... ELSE... ENDIF` structure supports only dichotomous (two-valued) choices: If the condition evaluates to `true`, the interpreter executes the `IF` part of the program. If the condition evaluates to **false**, the interpreter branches to the **ELSE** part of the program.

In reality, though, we are often required to choose among *many* alternative courses of action. Hence, we'd like the interpreter to be able to (1) evaluate a multi-valued (rather than a dichotomous) condition, and (2) depending on the resulting value of the condition, branch to one of several (rather than two) alternative courses of action. In dBASE, this branching mechanism is implemented through the **CASE** structure. Here is an example in which **CASE** comes handy:

> *MAIL ORDER* A mail-order company located in New York sells prints and posters over the telephone and ships them anywhere in the United States. The total cost of an order consists of the basic cost plus delivery cost. The delivery cost is determined according to the following schedule:

State	Cost
Connecticut	$ 2.50
New Jersey	5.00
Pennsylvania	7.50
Massachusetts	7.50
New York	0.00
Any other state	10.00

The following program, named **order**, implements this cost schedule:

```
01 * order
02 * compute the cost of delivery
03 PRIVATE cost,delivery,ctotal,state
04 INPUT "What is the item's cost? " TO cost
05 ACCEPT 'State destination? ' TO state
06 state=UPPER(state)
07 DO CASE
08    CASE state='CT'
09         delivery=2.5
10    CASE state='NJ'
11         delivery=5
```

```
12    CASE state='PA' .OR. state='MA'
13         delivery=7.5
14    CASE state='NY'
15         delivery=0
16    OTHERWISE
17         delivery=10
18 ENDCASE
19 ctotal=cost+delivery
20 ?
21 ? 'Total cost: $'+LTRIM(STR(ctotal))
22 RETURN
```

The following transcript demonstrates the program in action. The line numbers on the left side of each output line should help you keep track of the program's execution. They indicate which program lines were executed *before* that particular output line was displayed on the screen.

```
                    . do order
3,4                 What is the item's cost? 50
5                   State destination? NJ
6,7,8,10,11,
18,19,20,21         Total cost: $55

                    . do order
3,4                 What is the item's cost? 100
5                   State destination? dc
6,7,8,10,12,14,
16,17,18,19,20,21   Total cost: $110
```

The flow of control of the **order** program begins with lines 3, 4, 5, 6, and 7. Then, depending on the value of the variable **state**, the interpreter executes one, and *only* one, of the following commands: 9, 11, 13, 15, or 17. After executing one of these commands, the interpreter skips to the line following the **ENDCASE** key word, and the flow of control continues to lines 19, 20, 21, and 22.

Exercise 3-1 (1) Why is line 4 **INPUT** and line 5 **ACCEPT**? (2) What is the purpose of line 6? Be specific.

THE CASE SYNTAX

The syntax of the **CASE** structure is as follows:

```
DO CASE
   CASE <logical expression>
        <commands>
   .

   .

   .

   CASE <logical expression>
        <commands>
   OTHERWISE
        <commands>
ENDCASE
```

When the interpreter encounters a **CASE** structure, it starts to evaluate the logical expressions, one after the other. If one of the logical expressions evaluates to **true**, the interpreter executes its associated body of commands. Next, the interpreter skips the remainder of the **CASE** structure (even if some of the other logical expressions are also true), and goes on to execute the commands following the **ENDCASE** key word. If *all* the logical expressions are **false**, the interpreter executes the body of commands that follow the **OTHERWISE** key word.

The **OTHERWISE** clause is an optional feature of the **CASE** structure. In many situations, it is unnecessary. For example, if the **order** program were extended to specify a delivery cost for *every* state in the U.S.A., there would be no need for the **OTHERWISE** option. Recalling Murphy's Law, however, **OTHERWISE** would probably be useful in this case also: it would trap all the cases in which the user has entered a nonexistent state.

Warning The dBASE III PLUS interpreter is not perfect. If you forget to provide the mandatory **ENDCASE** line (a very common error), the interpreter will *not* issue an error message, and will go on to execute the program as if it were syntactically correct. This will cause unexpected program behavior that is very difficult to debug.

CASE AND IF

Note that anything that **CASE** can do, **IF** can also do. The resulting code, however, will be quite cumbersome. This is illustrated in the following program, which produces precisely the same results as the **order** program:

```
01 * order1
02 * compute the cost of delivery
03 PRIVATE cost,delivery,ctotal,state
04 INPUT "What is the item's cost? " TO cost
05 ACCEPT 'State destination? ' TO state
06 state=UPPER(state)
07 IF state='CT'
08    delivery=2.5
09 ELSE
10    IF state='NJ'
11       delivery=5
12    ELSE
13       IF state='PA' .OR. state='MA'
14          delivery=7.5
15       ELSE
16          IF state='NY'
17             delivery=0
18          ELSE
19             delivery=10
20          ENDIF
21       ENDIF
22    ENDIF
23 ENDIF
24 ctotal=cost+delivery
25 ?
26 ? 'Total cost: $'+LTRIM(STR(ctotal))
27 RETURN
```

Exercise 3-2   Examine the **order1** program, and convince yourself that it is indeed one hundred percent logically equivalent to the **order** program. You can do this by trying to hand-simulate both programs for, say, **state='PA'** and **state='CO'** (in separate runs). In other words, put yourself in the shoes of the interpreter, and try to execute both programs on these inputs.

Looping (WHILE)

Many business as well as scientific applications have an inherent *cyclical* nature: they involve doing the same thing (or something very similar) over and over again, until a certain *termination condition* is met. In programming lingo, this is called **looping**. To illustrate, consider the following two cases, which can't be solved without some sort of a looping mechanism:

> *PAYROLL* A payroll program prints monthly pay checks for all the employees of a large corporation. Basically, it is sufficient to teach the program how to print *one* check. Then it's just a matter of repeating this task over and over again, once for each record in the employees file. The program will keep printing checks until the **END OF FILE** (**EOF**) condition has been reached. Said otherwise, as long as, or **WHILE**, it is *not* **EOF**, the program will continue to process employees and print checks.

> *SUMMATION* A program is designed to input a series of numbers from a user and compute their sum. The situation is a bit tricky because we don't know in advance *how many* numbers the user would like to enter. The program gets around this problem by asking the user to terminate the data set with the number 0. Thus, if the user enters, say, the numbers 2, 3, 5, and 0, the program displays the output 10.

On the surface, the **payroll** and the **summation** programs have nothing in common. From a logical standpoint, though, they are very similar. To begin with, neither program knows in advance how many numbers (employees) it has to process. We thus keep adding numbers (processing checks) as long as, or **WHILE**, these numbers are non-zero (**EOF** has not been reached). Once a 0 (**EOF**) has been detected, processing must be terminated. This strategy can be described more precisely as follows:

```
(1) get the first input
(2) IF this is the end of the input, GOTO step (6)
(3) process this input
(4) get the next input
(5) GOTO step (2)
(6) end of loop
```

One key advantage of this loop is that it can handle a data set of any size, regardless of whether it consists of 3 or 3,000,000 numbers (employees). In dBASE, this very same loop is implemented through the more elegant **WHILE** structure, as follows:

```
get the first input
DO WHILE this is not the end of the input:
   process this input
   get the next input
ENDDO
```

The **WHILE** structure has two built-in, and hidden, **GOTO** commands that cause it to behave exactly the same as the six-step sequence. In particular, when the interpreter translates the **DO WHILE condition** command to machine language, it replaces it with the command **IF not(condition) GOTO addr1**, where **addr1** is the memory address of the command that follows the **ENDDO** key word. In a similar vein, the **ENDDO** key word is replaced by the command **GOTO addr2**, where **addr2** is the address of the command **IF not(condition) GOTO addr1**. This way, the interpreter transforms the high-level **WHILE** structure to the low-level six-step structure.

The words *high* and *low* in the last sentence refer to an abstract scale of comprehension. At the highest end of the scale there is human intelligence, or the way people structure their thoughts about problem solving. At the lowest end of the scale there are machine instructions—the only language that computers understand. High-level structures, like **WHILE**, enable programmers to describe problems in human terms, using a logical language that is easy to understand (after some training). Low-level commands, like **GOTO**, lend themselves to the robotic nature of machine language.

Since the interpreter does all the necessary translations from dBASE to machine language, structures like **WHILE** and **CASE** relieve the programmer from the tedium of using **GOTO** commands and line numbers. In fact, dBASE doesn't have a **GOTO** command at all! Other languages—like Fortran, Cobol, and Basic—are more "generous" in that respect; they allow programmers to use **GOTO** commands. It turns out however that this generosity is a mixed blessing: programs with many **GOTO**s tend to be convoluted, confusing, and difficult to follow. Such programs are typically referred to (unkindly) as *spaghetti code*.

We now return to the generic summation program (page 94), and show its dBASE implementation:

```
01 * sum
02 * sum up a series of numbers
03 PRIVATE msum,x
04 msum=0
05 INPUT 'Enter a number (or end with 0): ' TO x
```

```
06 DO WHILE x<>0
07     msum=msum+x
08     INPUT 'Enter a number (or end with 0): ' TO x
09 ENDDO
10 ?
11 ? 'The sum of this series is: '+LTRIM(STR(msum))
12 RETURN
```

The execution of **sum** is illustrated in the following transcript. As usual, the numbers on the left refer to line numbers in the program.

```
           . do sum
3,4,5      Enter a number (or end with 0): 30
6,7,8      Enter a number (or end with 0): 115
9,6,7,8    Enter a number (or end with 0): 20
9,6,7,8    Enter a number (or end with 0): 0
9,6,10,11  The sum of this series is: 165
```

THE WHILE SYNTAX

The general syntax of the **WHILE** structure is as follows:

```
DO WHILE <logical-expression>
        <commands>
ENDDO
```

In this syntax template, the **<commands>** label stands for one or more commands, and is typically referred to as the "body of the loop." The body of the loop will get executed as long as the logical expression (**x<>0** in the **sum** program) evaluates to **true**. When this expression evaluates to **false**, the interpreter will skip the body of the loop and continue to execute the commands following the **ENDDO** key word.

Warning The dBASE III PLUS interpreter is not perfect. If you forget to provide the mandatory **ENDDO** line (a very common error), the interpreter will *not* issue an error message, and will go on to execute the program as if it were syntactically correct. This will cause unexpected program behavior that is very difficult to debug.

Two important but optional features of the **WHILE** structure are the **EXIT** and the **LOOP** shortcuts:

EXIT: The **EXIT** command may be inserted anywhere in the body of the loop. When the interpreter encounters an **EXIT**, it terminates the loop and skips forward to execute the commands following the **ENDDO** line.

LOOP: The **LOOP** command may be inserted anywhere in the body of the loop. When the interpreter encounters a **LOOP**, it ignores the remainder of the body of the loop and skips backward to the **DO WHILE** line.

EXIT and **LOOP** are legitimate commands, but one should use them with restraint. Overusing these commands is considered bad taste, because they break the logical flow of the **WHILE** structure. When it comes to programming, elegance and style count dearly. Therefore, it is often better to write a few lines of code that will enable a **WHILE** loop to terminate naturally, rather than knocking it out abruptly with an **EXIT** clause.

The **WHILE** structure is *the* workhorse of structured programming. It is used in many different shapes and forms, and it pops up in almost every real-life program. The next five sections of this chapter give examples of how **WHILE** is used to do calculations, data analysis, data entry, text processing, and numeric analysis. These are just a few random (but highly illustrative) examples of the central role that **WHILE** plays in programming.

CALCULATING WITH WHILE

Consider the following definition of the *factorial function*—an important tool that is widely used in probability and statistics:

FACTORIAL FUNCTION The definition of the factorial function, denoted $n!$, is as follows: If $n = 0$ or $n = 1$, $n! = 1$. If $n > 1$, $n! = 1 \cdot 2 \cdot \ldots \cdot (n-1) \cdot n$.

To illustrate, 3! equals $1 \cdot 2 \cdot 3 = 6$, and 5! equals 120. The following program inputs a number from the user, and then goes on to compute and display its factorial:

```
01 * fact
02 * computes the factorial n! for an inputted n
03 PRIVATE n,fact,i
04 INPUT 'enter a number: ' TO n
05 fact=1
06 i=0
```

```
07 DO WHILE i<n
08    i=i+1
09    fact=fact*i
10 ENDDO
11 ? 'The factorial of '+LTRIM(STR(n))
12 ?? ' is '+LTRIM(STR(fact))
13 RETURN
```

Exercise 3-3   Write on paper the following commands, on three separate lines: **n=4**, **fact=1**, and **i=0**. Next, put yourself in the shoes of the interpreter and execute lines 7-12 of the **fact** program, changing the values of the variables on paper as you step through the loop. If you do it right, the value of the variable **fact** at the end of the exercise should be 24 (which is 4!).

Exercise 3-4   Test the **fact** program on **n=7**, **n=0**, and **n=-19** (in separate runs). Next, fix it so that it will refuse to run on negative inputs.

ANALYZING DATA WITH WHILE

In data analysis applications, one is often required to read a set of numbers and compute all sorts of statistics, like average, standard deviation, mean, minimum value, and maximum value. In this section, we focus on the last requirement, as follows:

> *MAXIMUM CALCULATIONS*   As part of several calculations you are asked to do on a large set of numbers, you are asked to find and print the largest number in the series.

This problem can be solved through a programming trick that, like other tricks, is much easier to perform once you've seen someone else do it:

```
01 * max
02 * finds the maximum number in a series of numbers
03 PRIVATE x,xmax
04 INPUT 'Enter a number (or end with 0): ' TO x
05 xmax=0
06 DO WHILE x<>0
07     IF x>xmax
08         xmax=x
```

```
09    ENDIF
10    INPUT 'Enter a number (or end with 0): ' TO x
11 ENDDO
12 ?
13 ? 'The maximum number is: '+LTRIM(STR(xmax))
14 RETURN
```

. DO max

1,2,3,4,5:	Enter a number (or end with 0):	123
6,7,8,9,10:	Enter a number (or end with 0):	5
11,6,7,9,10:	Enter a number (or end with 0):	17
11,6,7,8,9,10:	Enter a number (or end with 0):	526
11,6,7,9,10:	Enter a number (or end with 0):	98
11,6,7,9,10:	Enter a number (or end with 0):	0

11,6,12,13   The maximum number is: 526

The logic of this program is as follows: We assume that the largest number in the series is 0 (line 4). If we later encounter a number that is *greater* than the present maximum (line 7), we make *it* the new maximum (line 8). We then go on to read the next number, and so forth.

Exercise 3-5 Simulate the program on paper using the data set 4, 6, and 2. Then test it on the computer on the same data set. Next, test the program on the data set −193, −200, and −7. Note that the program produces a wrong output. Finally, fix the program so that it will print the right answer for *any* series of numbers, including (−193, −200, −7). Note: This exercise requires some thought. (Hint: Only one line must be changed in the program, and this line is *before* the WHILE loop.)

Exercise 3-6 Extend the xmax program so that it prints *both* the maximum *and* the minimum of any given series of numbers, using the same loop to do data entry and all the necessary calculations. Call the new program minmax.

DATA ENTRY WITH WHILE

Consider the following problem, which, at first sight, seems to have nothing to do with WHILE:

CONTROLLED DATA ENTRY (PART I) As part of a complex insurance application, a certain program is supposed to capture the
age of a policy holder. It is safe to assume that **age** will be
a positive number that doesn't exceed 200. Yet the data entry clerks who work with this program are not perfect. When
presented with the prompt **Enter age:**, they sometimes enter numbers like −19.5 and 5782. How can we deal with these
problems?

As it turns out, the design of error-free human/computer dialogs
can benefit greatly from the **WHILE** structure. The following program is
a case in point:

```
. do data_ent
Enter age: 358
*** Please be serious.
Enter age: -19.5
*** Please be serious.
Enter age: 56
Enter sex (m/f): what do you mean?
*** check yourself.
Enter sex (m/f): k
*** check yourself.
Enter sex (m/f): &*^5asdh
*** check yourself.
Enter sex (m/f): M

01 * data_ent
02 * inputs and validates age and sex data
03 *
04 INPUT 'Enter age: ' TO age
05 DO WHILE age<0 .OR. age>200
06    ? '*** Please be serious.'
07    INPUT 'Enter age: ' TO age
08 ENDDO
09 *
10 ACCEPT 'Enter sex (m/f): ' TO sex
11 sex=upper(sex)
12 DO WHILE .NOT.(sex='M' .OR. sex='F')
```

```
13    ? '*** check yourself.'
14    ACCEPT 'Enter sex (m/f): ' TO sex
15    sex=upper(sex)
16 ENDDO
17 RETURN
```

As you see, the two **WHILE** loops in **data_ent** serve as stubborn guards that refuse to let anything but good data enter the program. Shielding programs against garbage input is a key component of business applications, and the **data_ent** program illustrates a *generic testing strategy* that can be easily adapted to create a great variety of shields. Regardless of the input's type (and its specific validity test), the strategy always follows this form:

```
1. get the user's input
2  check the input
3. DO WHILE the input is no good
       display an error message
       get the user's input
       check the input
   ENDDO
   * at this point the input must be good
4. process the input
```

Exercise 3-7   Write a program that asks the user to enter an area code (three digits). The program must check that the entered area code is valid—that its middle digit is either 0 or 1. If the area code is invalid, the program must display an error message and ask the user to try again, and so forth. When the user enters a valid area code, the program should terminate its execution. Name the program **acode**. (Hint: Accept the area code as a string, and use string processing to focus on its middle digit.)

TEXT PROCESSING WITH WHILE

Consider the following problem:

> *TEXT COMPRESSION*   Textual data is full of "unnecessary" spaces. For example, each page in this book contains a great deal of white space. If we had to transmit this book via an expensive communications line, we could probably save some time and money by first deleting all its excessive spaces.

The following program, named **compress**, is designed to carry out this task. The program interacts with the user (and with other programs, as we'll see later) by using two global variables. The first variable—named **tin**—is assumed to contain the text that has to be compressed. The second variable—named **tout**—is where the program stores the compressed version of **tin**. The following transcript illustrates the program's execution:

```
. tin = 'Jill &      Jim    went down  the     hill'
. tout=''
. DO compress
. ? tout

Jill & Jim went down the hill
```

```
01 * compress
02 * Deletes repetitive spaces
03 * GLOBAL tin: input text to be compressed
04 * GLOBAL tout: compressed output
05 PRIVATE t,x
06 *
07 t=tin                    && make a copy of tin
08 tout=''                  && initialize tout
09 DO WHILE LEN(t)>0
10     x=LEFT(t,1)          && get the first char in t
11     t=RIGHT(t,LEN(t)-1)  && delete it from t
12     tout=tout+x          && and append it to tout.
13     IF x=' '             && if it's a SPACE, then
14        DO WHILE x=' '     && as long as x is SPACE
15           x=LEFT(t,1)      && get next char from t
16           t=RIGHT(t,LEN(t)-1)    && delete it from t
17        ENDDO
18        tout=tout+x        && append non-space to tout
19     ENDIF
20 ENDDO                     && check the next char in t
21 RETURN
```

Exercise 3-8 The **compress** program is quite challenging, and an excellent exercise might be to try to figure out how it works. First, read the program's documentation and get a general feel of what's going on. Next, assume that `tin='U.  S.   A.'` (that's two spaces after `'U.'` and three spaces after `'S.'`), and simulate the program's execution on paper, tracking the values of the variables **t**, **x**, and **tout** as you go along.

Exercise 3-9 Write a program, named **delspace**, that deletes all the spaces from a given variable **tin**. If you enter the four commands `tin='W    h        at      ?'`, `tout=''`, `DO delspace`, and `? tout`, you should get the output **What?**.

NUMERIC ANALYSIS WITH WHILE

The **WHILE** structure is always used in programs involving repetitive data processing. But don't get the impression that this is the only use of this structure. Practically every algorithm that contains a repetitive element must be implemented through **WHILE**, regardless of the context of the problem. This is illustrated in the following example:

> *PRIME NUMBERS* A prime number is a number that is divisible only by 1 and by itself. For example, 23 is a prime number. 323 is not a prime because it is divisible by 19. Can you think of a general method to find out whether a given number is a prime?

The simplest solution to this problem is to attempt to divide the number, say x, by $2, 3, 4, \ldots, x-1$. On a second thought, it is sufficient to limit the search to $2, 3, 4, \ldots, \sqrt{x}$. (Can you explain why?) If any of these numbers divides x, we'll announce that x is *not* a prime. If none of these numbers divides x, we'll announce that x *is* a prime.

One way to test whether x is divisible by y is to inspect the remainder of x/y. In dBASE, this remainder can be calculated through the expression **x/y-INT(x/y)**. If this expression is 0, **y** divides **x**. (Recall that the function **INT(x)** returns the integer part of **x**, e.g., **INT(3.75)** returns 3.) This strategy is implemented in the following program:

```
01 * prime
02 * checks if a given number is a prime
03 PRIVATE x,divider,limit,prime,remainder
04 INPUT 'Enter a number: ' TO x
05 limit=INT(SQRT(x))
06 divider=2
07 prime=.T.
```

```
08 DO WHILE divider<=limit
09    remainder=x/divider-INT(x/divider)
10    IF remainder=0
11       prime=.F.
12       EXIT
13    ENDIF
14    divider=divider+1
15 ENDDO
16 ? LTRIM(STR(x))
17 IF prime
18    ?? ' is a prime number'
19 ELSE
20    ?? ' is not a prime. It is divisible by '
21    ?? LTRIM(STR(divider))
22 ENDIF
23 RETURN
```

```
. do prime
Enter a number: 1747
1747 is a prime number

. do prime
Enter a number: 975119
975119 is not a prime. It is divisible by 367

. do prime
Enter a number: 10000079
10000079 is a prime number
```

Here is another prime number:

$$2^{127} - 1 = 170141118346046923173168730371588 4105727.$$

Before you rush to verify that $2^{127} - 1$ is a prime using the above program, consider the following fact: It took a 80386-based computer ninety seconds to step through the entire loop and find out that 10000079 is a prime number. It would take the same computer, running the same program, 30,000,000,000,000,000,000,000,000 *centuries* to discover that $2^{217}-1$ is a prime.

If we could run the same program on a super-computer that is a million times faster, we would still have to wait 10^{19} centuries (give or take a few billion years) until the program completes its execution and displays something on the screen. The lesson is clear: There exist difficult problems that cannot be solved by simply throwing hardware at them. What is needed here is not a better computer, but a better program.

The RETURN Command

We've already seen many examples of the **RETURN** command, which is used to terminate dBASE programs. This command looks like the programming equivalent of the familiar "That's all, folks!" banner, but there is a little more to it. First, the **RETURN** command can appear *anywhere* in a program. Second, the same program can have *several* **RETURN** commands. The following case illustrates an example that benefits from multiple **RETURN** commands:

> *LOGIN PROCEDURE* The Bit-N-Byte service is a computerized dating system available for people who have a personal computer, a modem, and a dream. For a monthly fee of $9.95, you get a password that enables you to "log in" and access a dating bulletin board. The password this month is *shishkebob*.

Here is how the login procedure works for an unauthorized user who tries to break into the system by entering random passwords:

```
. do login
Enter the password: tuna salad
      *** wrong password—try again
Enter the password: escargot
      *** wrong password—try again
Enter the password: hamburger
      ***   Three strikes and you're out   ***
```

As you see, the login procedure is cordial, up to a certain point, where it becomes nasty. It assumes the user may have simply forgotten the password, and it allows him or her three trials, after which it shuts itself off (similar to the way ATM machines work). Here is how the procedure works for a legitimate user:

```
. do login
Enter the password: shislik
```

```
*** wrong password—try again
Enter the password: shishkebob
***  Welcome to the Bit-N-Byte dating system  ***
```

The code of the **login** program, which has two exit points (two **RETURN** commands), is as follows:

```
01 * login
02 * a login procedure to a computerized dating service
03 *
04 PRIVATE password, response, ntrial
05 password='shishkebob'
06 ntrial=0
07 ACCEPT 'Enter the password: ' TO response
08 DO WHILE response<>password
09    ntrial=ntrial+1
10    IF ntrial<3
11       ? '*** wrong password—try again'
12    ELSE
13       ?
14       ? "***  Three strikes and you're out  ***"
15       RETURN
16    ENDIF
17    ACCEPT 'Enter the password: ' TO response
18 ENDDO
19 * at that point, the user must be legitimate.
20 ?
21 ? '***  Welcome to the Bit-N-Byte dating system  ***'
22 RETURN
```

According to the unwritten rules of programming etiquette, it is considered bad taste to have too many **RETURN**s in the same program. Some purists even argue that a program should have only one **RETURN** command, at the very end. The reason is that many **RETURN**s obscure the logic of an otherwise good program.

This rule is generally true, but there is no need to follow it religiously. The **RETURN** command in line 15 of the **login** program could have been eliminated by some additional programming, but the resulting code would be cumbersome and less readable.

Exercise 3-10   Suppose that line 15 in the **login** program was replaced with the command **EXIT**. What would be the impact of this change on the program's behavior?

Programs that Call Other Programs

All the mini-cases we've seen thus far were "solved" by means of a *single* program. In reality, complex systems consist of several interrelated programs that work in tandem on the same problem. This requires a mechanism that enables one program to "call," or **invoke**, other programs. In dBASE, this mechanism is implemented through the **DO** command.

The **DO** command can be used in two ways. If a user enters, say, **DO calc** from interactive mode, he or she instructs the interpreter to execute a program named **calc**. In precisely the same manner, a *program* (rather than a human user), can also invoke the **calc** program by using the very same command—**DO calc**. To illustrate, consider the following example.

Suppose we have two programs, named **main** and **calc**. The **main** program contains a line saying **DO calc**. When we enter **DO main** from interactive mode, the interpreter starts to execute the **main** program. When it encounters the line **DO calc** in **main**'s code, the interpreter freezes the execution of **main** and starts executing **calc**. When it encounters a **RETURN** in **calc**'s code, the interpreter exits **calc** and goes back to **calc**'s calling environment—the **main** program. It then proceeds to execute the command in **main**'s code that comes *immediately after* the line **DO calc**. When it encounters a **RETURN** in **main**'s code, the interpreter goes back to **main**'s calling environment—interactive mode.

The following case illustrates a problem and a solution that involves more than one program.

> *EMPLOYEE STATISTICS*   A company that is suspected of discriminatory hiring policies is asked to produce some key personnel statistics. Among other things, the company must provide (1) the average age of its employees, and (2) the male and female distribution of its work force. In reality, these data will be pulled out from a disk-based *file*. Since we haven't talked about files yet, let's assume the employee data are provided by a data-entry clerk.

Before we write this program, let's sketch its structure in "pseudo code." In what follows, the terms `age`, `sex`, `n`, `nmale`, `nfemale`, `sumage`, and `avg` are variable names.

```
set N, NMALE, and SUMAGE to 0
input and test the AGE and SEX of the next employee
DO WHILE this is not the end of the input:
    increase N by 1
    add the employee's AGE to SUMAGE
    IF it's a male
        increase NMALE by 1
    ENDIF
    input and test AGE and SEX of the next employee
ENDDO
set AVG to SUMAGE divided by N
set NFEMALE to N minus NMALE
print the values of AVG, NMALE, and NFEMALE
```

Exercise 3-11 Inspect the above program to be sure you understand its logic. Suppose you were required to extend the program so that it prints also the average ages of both males and females. How would you do it? Write your solution in pseudo code. (Hint: You will need more variables.)

Going back to the original program, let's focus on the pseudo command **input and test the AGE and SEX of the next employee**, which appears twice in the code. The dBASE translation of this command is quite elaborate: if we want to ensure that the **age** and **sex** data are good, we must test them through data-entry **WHILE** loops, as we've done in the **data_ent** program (page 100). But wait a minute. Given that we already have a program that knows how to enter and test sex and age data, why can't we simply enlist it to do this job for us? That's precisely what the following program does:

```
01 * process
02 * employee statistics
03 PRIVATE sumage,n,nmale,age,sex,avg
04 n=0
05 nmale=0
06 sumage=0
07 age=0
```

```
08 sex=''
09 *
10 DO data_ent        && get FIRST age and sex
11 DO WHILE age<>0
12    n=n+1
13    sumage=sumage+age
14    IF sex='M'
15       nmale=nmale+1
16    ENDIF
17    CLEAR
18    DO data_ent      && get NEXT age and sex
19 ENDDO
20 *
21 avg=sumage/n
22 ?
23 ? 'There are '+LTRIM(STR(nmale))+' males and '
24 ?? LTRIM(STR(n-nmale))+' females.'
25 ? 'The average age is: '+LTRIM(STR(avg,10,2))
26 RETURN
```

```
. do process
  Enter age: 39                  (data_ent, act I)
  Enter sex (m/f): m
  Enter age: 412                 (data_ent, act II)
  *** Please be serious.
  Enter age: 54
  Enter sex (m/f): f
  Enter age: 22                  (data_ent, act III)
  Enter sex (m/f): k
  *** check yourself.
  Enter sex (m/f): g
  *** check yourself.
  Enter sex (m/f): m
  Enter age: 0                   (data_ent, act IV)
  Enter sex (m/f): m
  There are 2 males and 1 females.
  The average age is: 38.33
```

Logically speaking, the pair of programs **process** and **data_ent** is completely equivalent to the following *single* program:

```
01 * process1
02 * employee statistics
03 PRIVATE sumage,n,nmale,age,sex,avg
04 n=0
05 nmale=0
06 sumage=0
07 *
08 INPUT 'Enter age: ' TO age      && get the first employee
09 DO WHILE age<0 .OR. age>200
10    ? '*** Please be serious.'
11    INPUT 'Enter age: ' TO age
12 ENDDO
13 *
14 ACCEPT 'Enter sex (m/f): ' TO sex
15 sex=upper(sex)
16 DO WHILE .NOT.(sex='M' .OR. sex='F')
17    ? '*** check yourself.'
18    ACCEPT 'Enter sex (m/f): ' TO sex
19    sex=upper(sex)
20 ENDDO
21 *
22 DO WHILE age<>0
23    n=n+1
24    sumage=sumage+age
25    IF sex='M'
26       nmale=nmale+1
27    ENDIF
28    CLEAR                       && clear the screen
29    *
30    INPUT 'Enter age: ' TO age  && get the next employee
31    DO WHILE age<0 .OR. age>200
32       ? '*** Please be serious.'
33       INPUT 'Enter age: ' TO age
34    ENDDO
35    *
```

```
36    ACCEPT 'Enter sex (m/f): ' TO sex
37    sex=upper(sex)
38    DO WHILE .NOT.(sex='M' .OR. sex='F')
39        ? '*** check yourself.'
40        ACCEPT 'Enter sex (m/f): ' TO sex
41        sex=upper(sex)
42    ENDDO
43 ENDDO
44 *
45 avg=sumage/n
46 ?
47 ? 'There are '+LTRIM(STR(nmale))+' males and '
48 ?? LTRIM(STR(n-nmale))+' females.'
49 ? 'The average age is: '+LTRIM(STR(avg,10,2))
50 RETURN
```

If a pair of programs achieves precisely the same result as a single, longer program, what's the advantage of writing two separate programs rather than one? The answer lies in the difference between **process** and **process1**. The former program is concise and readable, whereas the latter is convoluted and "out of focus"—you're not sure what exactly is going on.

As a rule, complex tasks are much easier to handle if they are divided into a series of smaller subtasks. **Modular programming**—the art of breaking up a complex system into smaller and more manageable modules—is a recommended practice for several reasons:

- Stand-alone programs can be developed simultaneously, by different people.

- Stand-alone programs can be tested simultaneously and independently from each other.

- If a program contains an error, the result is a local blunder rather than a global catastrophe. Local errors are much easier to detect and correct.

- Modular code reads well and is easy to understand. Therefore, modular code is easy to maintain and extend.

Here is one more example of how one program engages another program to accomplish a certain subtask:

CONTROLLED DATA-ENTRY (PART II)   Data-entry programs must cope with all sorts of hostile inputs. For example, some users have a tendency to press the spacebar several times between two consecutive words. This leads to cluttered files and wasted disk space. What's required is a program that scans the user's input and deletes all the excessive spaces.

We already know how to knock out unnecessary spaces from a given string via the **compress** program. The next transcript illustrates how this program can be used in the context of a larger application:

```
. do enter
Enter Name: Brandon  K.      Shmootznik  Jr.
Enter Address: 125   East 47  Street, New  York,  NY    10023
Name: Brandon K. Shmootznik Jr.
Address: 125 East 47 Street, New York, NY 10023
```

Even though you can't tell it from the transcript, **enter** is not working alone. Specifically, it interacts with **compress** via two variables: **tin** and **tout**. The first variable contains the text that has to be compressed; the second variable is where **enter** expects to find the result of the compression. The code is as follows:

```
01 * enter
02 * inputs name and address and compresses them
03 PRIVATE tin,tout
04 PRIVATE cname,caddr   && compressed name and address
05 *
06 tout=''
07 ACCEPT 'Enter Name: ' TO tin      && input name
08 DO compress                       && compress it
09 cname=tout
10 *
11 ACCEPT 'Enter Address: ' TO tin  && input address
12 DO compress                       && compress it
13 caddr=tout
14 ?
15 ? 'Name: '+cname                  && display the
16 ? 'Address: '+caddr               && compressed data
17 RETURN
```

The dBASE Interpreter as a Structured Program

To wrap up this chapter, it is fitting to note that the dBASE interpreter itself can be written using structured programming. Specifically, the general outline of this program is as follows:

```
display the dot prompt (.)
get the user's command
DO WHILE command <> 'QUIT'
    DO CASE
        CASE command='INPUT'
            DO input_routine
        CASE command='ACCEPT'
            DO accept_routine

            .
            .
            .

        OTHERWISE
            DO error_message_routine
    ENDCASE
    display the dot prompt (.)
    get the user's command
ENDDO
```

When you invoke dBASE, the interpreter begins to run by displaying the dot prompt. If the user enters the command **QUIT**, the interpreter terminates its execution. Otherwise, the interpreter inspects the user's command and branches to execute whatever the user wants to do. Hence, the **DO CASE** structure includes several hundred **CASE** sections—one for each legitimate dBASE command. If the command is illegitimate, the interpreter displays an error message. In any event, after the **CASE** structure is exited, the interpreter displays the next prompt, the user enters the next command, and so forth.

Variable Management

"Programming languages are built around the *variable*— its operations, control, and data structures" (Alan J. Perlis). Indeed, variables play a key role in programming; as you know by now, there is no way to write a serious program without putting a few variables to work. We conclude this chapter with a section on variable management in dBASE. Throughout the chapter we've used the terms **public**, **private**, and **global** quite casually. We now turn to define these variable types formally, giving advice on where, when, and how they should be used.

VARIABLES DECLARATION

If all you do in dBASE is write and execute one program at a time, it really doesn't matter how you handle your variables. If you declare them private at the beginning of the program, fine. If you don't declare them, no big deal. You can still use them any way you want. In fact, most dBASE books implicitly encourage the latter practice: "If a variable is not declared private," says one book, "it will be automatically treated as a private variable."

Indeed, many dBASE programmers don't bother to declare their variables through the **PRIVATE** command. It turns out that this is a very bad habit. As long as you play with one or two programs, it won't cause you much trouble. However, failure to declare variables in the context of a multi-program system might lead to catastrophic results, as it would enable some programs to unintentionally modify variables in other programs. These bugs are exceptionally notorious to deal with, especially if the programs were developed by different people.

Fortunately, all this trouble can be avoided if you take some simple preventive measures. This section gives you all the information that is necessary to make clever and safe use of dBASE variables. There is no need to memorize these rules, but it's important to practice them. If you are designing a complex system involving several programs, you will find this section to be a useful source of reference and therapeutic advice.

VARIABLES TERMINOLOGY

dBASE recognizes two types of variables: *public* and *private*. Public variables remain in effect throughout the entire dBASE session. Private variables are active as long as the program that declared them is running. When a program terminates its execution, all its private variables vanish into thin air.

The following three concepts might be useful in understanding how private and public variables work:

Declaration: A variable **x** is said to be *declared* when it is introduced to the interpreter through one of the commands **PUBLIC x** or **PRIVATE x**.

Initialization: A variable **x** is said to be *initialized* when it is assigned a value for the first time. Variables may be initialized through an assignment command (e.g., **x=17**), an **INPUT** command (e.g., **INPUT 'enter age:' TO x**), or an **ACCEPT** command (e.g., **ACCEPT 'enter name:' TO x**).

"Beyond": A program **p** is said to be *beyond* a program **q** if (1) **p** contains a line saying **DO q**, or (2) **p** contains a line saying **DO r**, and **r** is beyond **q**. In other words, **p** is said to be beyond **q** if the execution of **p** will trigger, at some point of time, the execution of **q**.

Multi-program systems form a hierarchy of "beyond" relationships. At the top of the hierarchy is one program that has no other program beyond it. This program is typically called the **main** or the **root** program. The main program is invoked from interactive mode.

THE RULES OF THE GAME

We are now in a position to give formal descriptions of four commands that are involved in the creation and deletion of dBASE variables:

PUBLIC: The command **PUBLIC x** instructs the interpreter to create a new variable called **x**. This variable will become accessible to *any* program subsequently invoked in the present dBASE session. *All* the variables initialized in interactive mode are public by default.

PRIVATE: The command **PRIVATE x**, given at the beginning of a program, say **prog1**, is a *passive* declaration statement. Unlike the **PUBLIC** command, it doesn't create anything. Instead, it tells the interpreter that *if* a variable named **x** will be *later* initialized somewhere in that program, then this variable should "belong" to **prog1**. This variable should have no relation whatsoever to any private or public variable named **x** that was declared in any program *beyond* the level of **prog1**.

Assignment: Suppose an initialization command, say **x=10**, was encountered by the interpreter somewhere in the code of a program called **prog1**. Suppose further that **x** was previously declared private in **prog1**. This will cause the interpreter to create a new variable, **x**, which will "belong" to **prog1**. Suppose now that **x** was *not* previously declared in **prog1**. In that case, the occurrence of the command **x=10** in **prog1** tells the interpreter the following story: "If a variable named **x** does not exist in any program beyond **prog1**, then go ahead and create it as private at the level of **prog1**. If, however, a variable named **x** *does* exist somewhere in a program beyond

prog1, then set the value of *that* variable to 10. In the latter case, no new variable will be created.

RETURN: This command instructs the interpreter to (1) terminate the execution of the present program, and (2) delete all its private variables from memory.

Exercise 3-12   Clyde McBug is part of a team of programmers that develops a financial advisory system consisting of forty-seven different programs. Clyde is asked to write a program, named **calc_net**, that calculates the net income of a user. In his program, Clyde enters the command **net=income*(1-tax)**, but he doesn't bother to declare **PRIVATE net** (**income** and **tax** are global variables in his program). What kind of a problem can Clyde create? Be specific, and give an example.

HOW TO USE VARIABLES IN dBASE

Now that you know the rules of the game, here is how you should play to win:

■ *Avoid public variables*: Contrary to the general opinion, there is absolutely no need to use public variables in dBASE. If you want a variable to be globally accessible throughout your system, declare it private in the root program of that system. If you want to restrict the exposure of this variable to a limited subset of programs, declare it private in the root program of this subset. When it comes to public variables, remember three things: don't use them; don't use them; don't use them. The only exception is testing. If you wish to test a program that manipulates one or more **GLOBAL** variables, you'll have to initialize these variable in interactive mode before you **DO** the program. This will create a bunch of public variables, but they will be used strictly for testing purposes.

■ *Declare thy variables*: All the variables mentioned in your program must be clearly documented at the top of the program. Suppose a certain program, say **calc**, manipulates two variables, **x** and **y**. Assume that **x** is used only locally, in **calc**, whereas **y** belongs to another program that is beyond **calc**. Both variables must be declared at the top of **calc**, as follows: (1) declare **x** private through the command **PRIVATE x**, and (2) declare **y** *global* through the comment *** GLOBAL y**. Even though this comment is *not* part of the dBASE syntax, it is a crucial note that will help you keep track of your variables. To sum up, you must document each variable in your program by using either a **PRIVATE** command or a *** GLOBAL** comment.

■ *Initialize thy variables*: Suppose the program **main** is beyond the program **calc**. Suppose **main** has a private variable called **x**. If you want **calc** to change the value of **x**, *be sure to initialize **x** in **main** before you invoke **calc***. If you forget to initialize **x** in **main**, you will fall victim to Murphy's Law. When the interpreter will encounter a command that assigns a value to **x** in **calc**, it will make **x** a private variable in **calc**. When **calc** terminates its execution, **x** will be wiped out of memory, and the link between **main** and **calc** will accompLish nothing.

Additional Exercises

Note: The first two exercises review Chapter 2 material. They can be solved without the use of **IF**, **CASE**, and **WHILE** structures.

3-13 Write a program that computes the future value of a savings program that pays interest *every week*. Ask the user how much money he or she wishes to invest, for how many years, and at what *annual* interest rate, as a percentage. Then use this information to compute and display the future value of the investment. Test the program on the following data: $1,000, invested for 5 years, at 12% annual interest. (Note: the weekly rate is the annual rate divided by 52.) Can you explain why banks prefer to pay interest annually rather than weekly? Name the program **wrate**.

3-14 Here's a little number-juggling trick. Ask a user for his or her birth year (two digits only, say 54 instead of 1954), and his or her age (two digits only, say 37). Then double the birth year and add five. Next, multiply the result by 50, add the age, and subtract 250. Finally, divide the result by 100. Then display the outcome on the screen *with two digits after the decimal point* (using **STR**). The result might surprise you. (Hint: Your program should use a single numeric expression to carry out this calculation, and this expression will have two pairs of round parentheses.) Name the program **juggle**, and test it on yourself.

3-15 Improve the **tarea** program (exercise 2-25, page 79) in the following way. For every three numbers that the user enters, the program must first figure out whether or not these numbers form a triangle. One way to detect this is to test if the number under the square root is positive. If it's either less than or equal to 0, the program must print the message **These numbers do not form a triangle.** Name the program **tarea1**, and test it on the same inputs as in the previous exercise.

3-16 Improve the **tarea1** program (see the previous exercise) in the following way. The new program must allow the user to enter as many data sets as he or she desires, and for each data set compute the respective triangle area. The process should be programmed to terminate when the user enters the special input $(0, 0, 0)$. Test your program on the following data sets: $(7, 5, 9)$, $(4, 12, 0)$, $(12, 9, 5)$, $(4, 2, 8)$, $(15, 12, 8)$, $(8, 15, 12)$, and $(0, 0, 0)$ (the parentheses and the commas are not part of the user's input). Name the program **tarea2**.

3-17 Write a program that inputs a list of names of students and their corresponding course grades (numbers between 0 and 100) and produces some statistics about the grades distribution. The overall logic of the program consists of a **DO WHILE** loop that terminates when the user enters the special student name **end**, followed by the special grade **0**. The outline of this loop is as follows:

```
ACCEPT name
INPUT x
DO WHILE name<>'end'
    do all sort of calculations with x (the grade)
    ACCEPT name
    INPUT x
ENDDO
```

Grades that are either greater than 100 or less than 0 must be rejected with an appropriate error message. At the end of its execution, the program must print the following information: number of students (people with valid grades), the name and grade of the student with the highest grade, the name and grade of the student with the lowest grade, the average class grade, the variance of the class grades, the number of students whose grades were greater than 74, the number of students whose grades were between 50 and 74 (inclusive), and the number of students whose grades were 49 or less.

Hints: You'll need a few variables—one for each calculation. For example, you will need a variable, say **count1**, where you store the number of students whose grades are greater than 74. The formulas of the average and variance of a list of numbers $x_1, \ldots, x_n$ are $avg = \frac{1}{n} \sum_{i=1}^{n} x_i$ and $var = \frac{1}{n} \sum_{i=1}^{n} (x_i)^2 - avg^2$.

Note that in order to compute the variance you'll need a variable that, for each grade **x** that the user provides, accumulates the sum of **x*x**. Name the program **grades**, and test it on the following data set: Steve, 50, Tom, 99, Joe, 102, Joe, 100, Jane,

98, Mike, −3, Mike, 30, Kim, 35, Paul, 86, Lisa, 28, Hal, 65, Al, 12, Joel, 78, Frank, 77, end, 0. Note 1: The user will enter the name and the age in two separate lines. Note 2: **Average**, **sum**, **count**, and **total** are reserved words in dBASE. You can't use them as variable names.

3-18 Write a program that computes the square root of a number **x** without using dBASE's built-in **SQRT(x)** function. This can be done through the following numeric method, discovered by Newton: If **y** is an approximation of $\sqrt{x}$, then $(x/y + y)/2$ is a better approximation of $\sqrt{x}$. This ingenious trick is applied repetitively, as follows: Start off by setting **y** to 1. Then check if **y** is close enough to $\sqrt{x}$, which is the same as checking if **y*y** is close enough to **x**. If it's not close enough, set **y** to **(x/y+y)/2**, and again check if **y*y** is now close enough to **x**. If it's not close enough, set **y** to **(x/y+y)/2**, and so on. This logic can be implemented by a **DO WHILE** loop that is programmed to terminate when **y*y** is close enough to **x**. To be concrete, let's decide that they are close enough when $|x - y \cdot y| \le 0.001$.

Start the program by inputing **x**. If **x** is negative, terminate the program with an appropriate message. If **x** is 0, the answer is 0. Otherwise, set **y** to 1 and go to work. When the loop terminates, announce **y** as the answer. Recall that the mathematical operator *absolute value of x* or $|x|$ is implemented in dBASE through the function **ABS(x)**. Name the program **newton**, and test it (in separate runs) on 4, 9, 0, −12, 36, and 15.

3-19 Write a program to train a first-grader how to add one- or two-digit integers. The program should give the user a series of random addition exercises, such as **12+7=?**, **13+32=?**, and so on. For each exercise, if the user answers correctly, the program should (1) say something nice, and (2) see if the user wants to continue. If the user provides a wrong answer, the program must repeat the last exercise, using the *same numbers*, until the user answers correctly.

Your program must be written so that it supports precisely the following style of interaction. (The user's input is shaded. The rest of the transcript is written by the program. The actual numbers that *your* program will generate might be different.)

```
Please enter your name:  Phil
Hi Phil.  I will now give you a few exercises.
----------------------------------------------
The sum of 23 and 52 is:  75
Good job, Phil !!
```

```
Would you like to try another exercise?  yes
------------------------------------------------
The sum of 75 and 13 is:   88
Good job, Phil !!
Would you like to try another exercise?  yes
------------------------------------------------
The sum of 12 and 17 is:   36
Wrong.  Try again.
------------------------------------------------
The sum of 12 and 17 is:   29
Good job, Phil !!
Would you like to try another exercise?  no
**********************************************
Thank you, Phil.  See you later.
```

(Note that the last line is ******** rather than ----). Name the program **tutor**, and test it by giving yourself a few addition exercises, printing the results as you go along. Make sure your test is complete.

Hints: You can generate a one- or two-digit random number by invoking a program called **random**, as follows. Every time you enter **DO random**, the program returns a random number in a global variable named **rnd**. Before you invoke it the first time, though, you must initialize **rnd** to a certain number, say 50000. The code of the program is as follows:

```
* random
* This program generates a one-digit or a
* two-digit random number and stores it
* in the global variable RND. This variable
* (RND) must be initialized to a seed value
* before the first time the program is called.
* GLOBAL rnd
rnd=MOD(13*rnd+7,31)
RETURN
```

The overall logic of the **tutor** program is as follows:

```
PRIVATE rnd,mcont,x1,x2,answer
rnd=50000
```

```
mcont=1
DO WHILE mcont=1
  . DO random        && put a random number in x1
    x1=rnd
    DO random        && put a random number in x2
    x2=rnd
    answer=0
    DO WHILE answer=0
       give the exercise with x1 and x2
       if the answer is correct, set answer to 1
       ENDIF
    ENDDO
    ask the user if s/he wants to continue
    if s/he says no, set mcont to 0
ENDDO
```

## CHAPTER FOUR

Building a System

In previous chapters we've seen many examples of independent, stand-alone programs, each designed to solve a self-contained and isolated problem. We now turn to describe the art of building a **system**—a set of interrelated programs and files that supports a wholesome business application like inventory control, airline reservations, or online banking.

Complex systems are typically built by several people. Therefore, it's important to know how to break them into well-defined **modules** that can be developed and tested separately and independently. Building a modular architecture is an important element of what is called **systems analysis and design**. In this chapter we focus on the point where systems analysis ends and programming begins—a point where system specifications are translated into computer programs. This critical stage will be demonstrated in the context of a familiar application: an automatic teller machine (ATM) system.

It is sometimes argued that programming is passé, and that systems can be built by **application generators**—programs that automatically convert system specifications into code. As it turns out, however, application generators are primarily effective in the examples that are used to demonstrate them. Although they can help cut down development time and cost, they are far from a total replacement of no-nonsense programming. If you've gone through Chapters 1, 2, and 3, you possess a good set of programming tools. We now proceed to put these tools together and build something new and exciting—a *system*.

The ATM System

During the last decade, automatic teller machines (ATMs) have become a permanent fixture of American banks. These machines enable customers to withdraw, deposit, and transfer funds electronically, without the assistance of a human teller. The various services that ATMs offer can be described pictorially, as shown in Figure 1.

The user interface of the ATM is **menu-driven**: after establishing access to the system, you are given a menu of options—withdraw, deposit, transfer, and so on. Each of these selections leads to a submenu, all the way down to a point where you actually transact business. Although ATMs vary from one bank to another, they all offer at least the basic services outlined in Figure 1. We now proceed to build a prototype ATM that simulates these services in dBASE. But first, let's pause to think about the general notion of automatic service machines.

Exercise 4-1 Compare the working of an ATM to that of a human teller. Do you think human tellers will be necessary in the 2000s? Why or why not?

Exercise 4-2 Reflect briefly on what would be the ATM equivalent in the following lines of business: film processing, dry cleaning, and fast food. Assume that all these services accept credit cards.

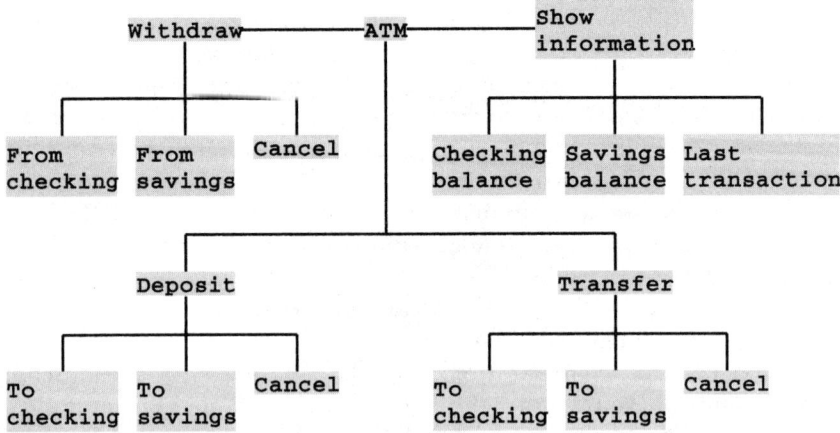

Figure I The ATM Menu Tree

The System's Architecture

The system architecture of our ATM prototype was designed through a process called *stepwise refinement* or *top-down design*. Beginning with the user's view of the ATM (Figure 1), we broke the overall system into individual modules and programs, ending up with Figure 2. Although we don't have space to describe the details of this process, we wish to emphasize that the architecture that emerged from it (Figure 2) is not arbitrary. Rather, it is based on a solid discipline of building menu-driven business applications.

Note that Figure 2 is an expansion of Figure 1. The nine modules on the periphery of Figure 1—**from-checking, from-savings ... last-transaction**—are each implemented by a single program in Figure 2. The four modules above this level—**withdraw, deposit, transfer**, and **info**—are implemented by two programs. The root of the system—the **atm** module—is implemented by four programs.

In addition to the program names, Figure 2 defines the *order* in which the various programs call each other. In particular, a right-bound link leading from, say, **program1** to **program2** indicates that the code of **program1** includes one line that reads **DO program2**. When **program2** terminates its execution, the flow of control returns to **program1**

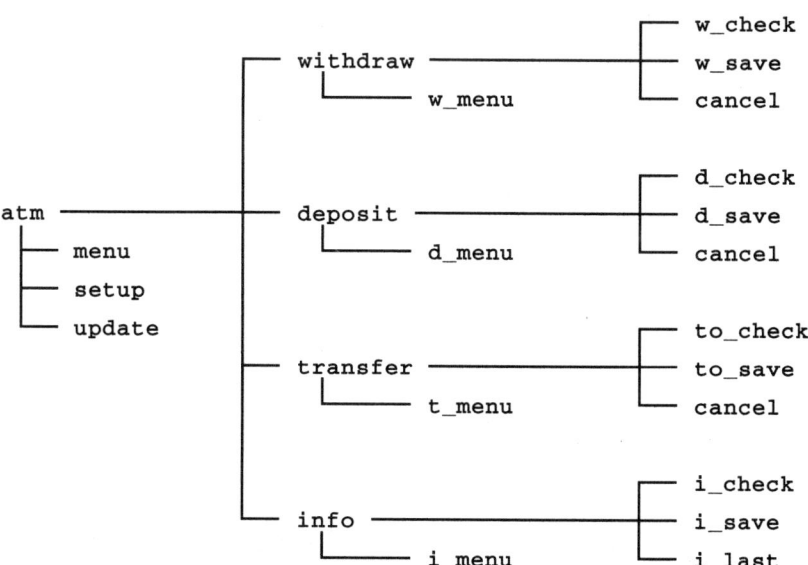

Figure 2 The ATM System Architecture

and eventually all the way up to the root program—**atm**. Since the system's architecture is a *hierarchy*, and the user interface is structured as a menu **tree**, everything fits in very nicely.

From a technical standpoint, the programs that make up the system can be divided into the following three categories:

- User Interface Drivers: These programs implement the menu-driven interface of the entire system. They include **atm**, **menu**, **withdraw**, **w_menu**, **deposit**, **d_menu**, **transfer**, **t_menu**, **info**, and **i_menu**.

- Functional Programs: These are the workhorses—programs that actually get things done. They include **w_check**, **w_save**, **d_check**, **d_save**, **to_check**, **to_save**, **i_check**, **i_save**, **i_last**, and **cancel**.

- Utilities: Utility programs serve other programs (rather than the ultimate user). The ATM system has two such programs: **setup** and **update**.

Exercise 4-3   In this exercise you are asked to get acquainted with our ATM prototype. Walk through the menus, try some deposit and withdrawal transactions, and get a general feeling of how the system works. The prototype is stored in the book's data disk under a subdirectory called **atm**. To use it, follow these steps: (1) enter the **DOS** command **CD atm**, (2) invoke dBASE, and (3) enter the command **DO atm**. Note that each time you invoke the system, you start with a zero balance. This convention is quite useful for testing purposes; later in the chapter we'll make it more realistic.

The User Interface

It is difficult to overemphasize the importance of the *human factor* in software design. Many great systems have failed in the marketplace because their designers forgot that they will be used by people other than the programmers who wrote them. This is particularly true in the case of ATMs—a product whose target customers consist mostly of novice users. If you are not sure what the term *novice user* means, consider the following example:

> *NOVICE USERS* Aunt Mimi is a fifty-five-year old salesclerk in a large New York department store. Although she has twelve years of education and thirty years of work experience behind the cash register, the thought of using computers gives her the chills. A few weeks ago she overheard her nephew say

something about dBASE, but she thought he was referring to a new spray against cockroaches. (Little did she know that this thing *creates* bugs rather than eliminates them.)

In order to transform our ATM prototype into an attractive product that *anybody* can use, we must wrap it up with a user-friendly interface. Now, the term *user-friendly* has become meaningless, as every software product describes itself that way. With that in mind, we offer the following formal definition of a **user-friendliness test**—a test that we recommend you apply to *any* business-oriented piece of software:

The User-Friendliness Test   When you think you are finished writing and testing a system, ask yourself the following question: *Can Aunt Mimi use it?* If the answer is no, the system is not user-friendly. If the answer is yes, give the system to Aunt Mimi and verify that she can really use it. You can always apply this test because regardless of where you work, if you look around you'll see one or two Aunt Mimis. Make sure to include them in your system design process, as they may well become the most important members on your team.

For one reason or another, one language that novice users understand well is the language of *menus*. Show them a menu, and they will know what to order. This is very fortunate, because a hierarchy of menus and submenus can be easily implemented in software, as we have done in our own ATM system. This user interface is demonstrated in the following session, which you are welcome to repeat on your computer:

```
. do atm
Please enter your PIN number: 7362

                Main ATM Menu
                -------------
        1: get cash
        2: deposit funds
        3: transfer funds
        4: see information
        0: exit
Enter your choice: 2
How much do you want to deposit? $1000
Where should the $1000 go to?
                1: To checking
                2: To savings
                3: Cancel
```

```
Enter your choice: 1
You deposited $1000
Your new checking balance is $1000
          Main ATM Menu
          -------------
          1: get cash
          2: deposit funds
          3: transfer funds
          4: see information
          0: exit
Enter your choice: 3
How much do you want to transfer? $700
What kind of transfer?
          1: From checking to savings
          2: From savings to checking
          3: Cancel
Enter your choice: 1
You transferred $700
from checking to savings
          Main ATM Menu
          -------------
          1: get cash
          2: deposit funds
          3: transfer funds
          4: see information
          0: exit
Enter your choice: 4
What would you like to see:
          1: Balance of checking account
          2: Balance of savings account
          3: Last transaction
          4: Main menu
Enter your choice: 3
Your last transaction was on 11/20/92
You transferred $700
from checking to savings
What would you like to see:
```

```
         1: Balance of checking account

         2: Balance of savings account

         3: Last transaction

         4: Main menu
Enter your choice: 4

         Main ATM Menu

         -------------

         1: get cash

         2: deposit funds

         3: transfer funds

         4: see information

         0: exit
Enter your choice: 1
How much do you want to withdraw? $350
From where should I take the $350?

         1: From checking

         2: From savings

         3: Cancel
Enter your choice: 1
You withdrew $350 from your checking account.
Your new checking account balance is $-50

         Main ATM Menu

         -------------

         1: get cash

         2: deposit funds

         3: transfer funds

         4: see information

         0: exit
Enter your choice: 0
```

As you see, the internal structure of the ATM system (Figure 2) is completely transparent. The user perceives the system as *one* program, invoked by the magic words **DO atm**. When **atm** begins its execution, a custom-made user interface takes over and controls all the interaction between the user and the computer. This interface will be in effect until the user exits the **atm** program, at which point the standard user interface of dBASE (the dot prompt) resumes.

It's a good exercise to try to "map" the session's progression on Figure 2. The entry point to the system is the **atm** program (the root of the hierarchy), which, among other things, displays the main menu. From the main menu, the user can branch to four alternative submenus, and so on. The remainder of this section presents four of the ten programs that facilitate this style of interaction. The remaining six programs are very similar in spirit and execution, and they are left for you as an exercise.

```
01 * atm
02 * called from: interactive mode
03 PRIVATE found,response
04 found=.F.
05 DO setup                && retrive user's record
06 IF found                && if found, go to work
07    response=0
08    DO menu               && invoke the main menu
09    DO WHILE response<>0  && RESPONSE = user's choice
10       DO CASE
11          CASE response=1
12             DO withdraw     && withdraw module
13          CASE response=2
14             DO deposit      && deposit module
15          CASE response=3
16             DO transfer     && funds transfer module
17          CASE response=4
18             DO info         && information module
19       ENDCASE
20       DO menu              && invoke main menu
21    ENDDO                   && loop to next transaction
22    DO update               && update customer's record
23 ELSE
24    ? ' *** access denied ***'      && bad pin routine
25 ENDIF
26 RETURN                     && exit to interactive mode
```

```
01 * menu
02 * called by: atm
03 * GLOBAL response
```

```
04 CLEAR
05 TEXT
06
07          Main ATM Menu
08          -------------
09          1: get cash
10          2: deposit funds
11          3: transfer funds
12          4: see information
13          0: exit
14
15 ENDTEXT
16 response=100
17 DO WHILE response<0 .OR. response>4
18    INPUT 'Enter your choice: ' TO response
19 ENDDO
20 RETURN
```

```
01 * deposit
02 * called by: atm
03 PRIVATE response,msum
04 ?
05 INPUT 'How much do you wish to deposit: $' TO msum
06 response=0
07 DO d_menu                && display the deposit menu
08 DO CASE                  && go to work
09    CASE response=1
10        DO d_check        && deposit to checking
11    CASE response=2
12        DO d_save         && deposit to savings
13    CASE response=3
14        DO cancel         && cancel the transaction
15        RETURN
16    ENDCASE
17 DO wait                  && delay routine
18 RETURN
```

```
01 * d_menu
02 * called by: deposit
03 * GLOBAL: msum, response
04 CLEAR
05 ?
06 ? 'Where should the $'+LTRIM(STR(msum))+' go to?'
07 TEXT
08
09              1: To checking
10              2: To savings
11              3: Cancel
12
13 ENDTEXT
14 response=100
15 DO WHILE response<0 .OR. response>3
16    INPUT 'Enter your choice: ' TO response
17 ENDDO
18 RETURN
```

The **TEXT ... ENDTEXT** feature is a new dBASE structure that we haven't seen yet. This structure allows you to display text (one or more lines) on the screen without using the display command **?**. This is a good way to display menus, because as far as the interpreter is concerned, a menu is nothing more than a bunch of text lines.

Exercise 4-4 Inspect the ATM session on page 127. Read the code of **atm**, **menu**, **deposit**, and **d_menu**, and try to understand how the *first* transaction of the user got executed (the deposit of $1,000). Important notes: (1) At this stage you are asked to ignore lines 1-7 in the **atm** program. In other words, start simulating the program (in your mind) from line 8. In a similar vein, ignore the line **Please enter your PIN number:** in the transcript. We'll take care of this procedure later. (2) Don't try to simulate the session beyond the point where the user selects option 1 from the deposit submenu. At that stage you will have to refer to programs you haven't seen yet.

Exercise 4-5 In preparation for the next sections, please print on paper *all* the programs that make up the ATM system, as follows: (1) change to the **atm** subdirectory on your data disk; (2) invoke dBASE; and (c) use **DO lprint** to print the programs **atm, menu, withdraw, deposit, transfer, info, w_menu, w_check, w_save, cancel, d_menu, d_check, d_save, t_menu, to_check, to_save, i_menu, i_check, i_save, i_last, setup, update, wait,** and **notyet**. That's twenty-four programs and twenty-four sheets of paper!

The Accounts File

The heart and soul of a real ATM system is a huge disk-based file that keeps track of the account balances of all the bank's customers. To illustrate, consider the following snapshot of a typical **accounts** file:

name	pin	cbal	sbal	credit	lastsum	lastop	lastdate
Lisa	6235	5500	1200	2500	300	wc	11/01/92
Paul	7736	-900	0	5000	500	ds	10/14/92
Ron	1234	900	1200	0	1000	cs	11/12/92
Tom	3342	200	3000	2000	700	sc	10/23/92

Although we have no space to cover files here, note that there is nothing mysterious about them. Stored on magnetic disks that retain data permanently, files are conceptually *tables* of unlimited size. There might be an **accounts** file, an **employees** file, a **stocks** file, and so on. The columns of the table (which vary from one file to another) are called **fields**, and the rows are called **records**. Each record is essentially a set of field values, or constants.

The names and types of the fields are not arbitrary. Like the rest of the system's architecture, they emerged from an elaborate requirements analysis that translated the needs of users (in this case bank customers and personnel) into concrete file specifications. In our own ATM system, the rules of the game were set as follows. The **name** field stores the customer's name. The **pin** field stores the secret personal identification number that enables entry to the customer's accounts. **cbal** and **sbal** store the current balances of the customer's checking and savings accounts. **credit** stores the credit limit, which varies from one customer to another. This number specifies how much money the bank is willing to lend the customer. For example, consider Tom: given his present balances, he will be able to withdraw as much as $5,200, but not more.

The last three fields store the details of the customer's *last* transaction. `lastsum` records how much money was transacted. `lastop` records the transaction type, which is either **wc** (withdraw from checking), **ws** (withdraw from savings), **dc** (deposit to checking), **ds** (deposit to savings), **cs** (transfer from checking to savings), or **sc** (transfer from savings to checking). Finally, `lastdate` records the date of the last transaction.

Putting It All Together

The overall logic of the ATM system can be described in the following procedure, written in pseudocode:

```
1. Input the customer's secret PIN number
2. Search the ACCOUNTS file for a record
   with such a PIN number
3. IF such a record was found:
        3.1 copy its field values to
            memory-based variables;
        3.2 let the customer execute all his/her
            transactions (this might take a little
            while), and change the balances and
            last transaction variables accordingly;
        3.3 when the customer is done, update his
            or her record by copying the variable
            values to their respective fields,
            and exit the system.
   ELSE
       deny access to the system
   ENDIF
```

Since file management is not covered in this book, our ATM prototype focuses "only" on stage 3.2, which actually amounts to about ninety percent of the overall ATM system. Stages 1, 2, and 3.1 are *simulated* in our system by the following program:

```
01 * setup
02 * called from: atm
03 * initializes global variables to default values
```

```
04 PUBLIC mpin,mcbal,msbal,mlim,mlastsum,mlastop,mlastdate
05 * GLOBAL found (initialized to .F. by atm)
06 *
07 INPUT 'Please enter your PIN number: ' TO mpin
08 found=.T.               && assume the record was found
09 mcbal=0                 && checking balance
10 msbal=0                 && savings balance
11 mlim=2500               && credit limit
12 mlastsum=0              && last sum transacted
13 mlastop=''              && last transaction type
14 mlastdate=CTOD(' / / ') && date of last transaction
15 RETURN
```

As you see, the **setup** program is quite minimal. The **pin** number is entered merely for special effects, as the program happily proceeds to work with *any* user-supplied input. In fact, the program makes no attempt to access any file, and instead of copying the customer's data from his or her record onto variables, it initializes these variables to null values (with the exception of **mlim**, which assumes that all customers get a $2,500 credit line). Thanks to this procedure, every test of the ATM system begins with a clean slate of balances and last transaction information. (Note that the variables are declared **PUBLIC**. This is done strictly for testing purposes. Later in the chapter we'll make these variables **PRIVATE** at the **atm** level.)

Stage 3.3 is simulated in our system by a program named **update**, which, embarrassing as it may be, consists of one line of code: **RETURN**. Recall that this program is supposed to post the new balances onto the customer's record. Since the present version of the system employs no files, there is nothing to update:

```
01 * update
02 * called by: atm
03 * This program is invoked only once, at the end
04 * of the ATM session, after the user has completed
05 * all his or her transactions. Before we terminate
06 * the session, we must post the new balances (which
07 * are presently stored in variables) in the user's
08 * record. This is done by copying the values of the
09 * global variables MCBAL, MSBAL, MLASTSUM, MLASTOP,
10 * and MLASTDATE onto their respective fields in the
```

```
11 * user's record.
12 * NOTE: This module is presently not implemented.
13 RETURN
```

Additional Exercises

In the remainder of this chapter we will complete the ATM system, which at present is only fifty percent operational. In the process, you'll be asked to edit nine programs that are already stored on the data disk. Instead of code, these programs contain *comments* that explain their desired operations. In addition, each program declares a set of variables, so there is no need to introduce any new variables to the system. Some programs include the command **DO notyet**. This trivial program displays the message **This module is not yet implemented**. Obviously, this message must be removed after the program has been completed.

Exercises 4-6 to 4-9 are an integral part of this chapter, and we strongly recommend that you complete them. Exercises 4-10 to 4-14 are optional, as they require knowledge of file processing in dBASE.

4-6 Complete the **d_save** program, using **d_check** as a model. Don't forget to record the last transaction information in the variables **mlastsum**, **mlastop**, and **mlastdate**. This will complete the deposit module of the ATM.

4-7 Complete the programs **withdraw**, **w_menu**, **w_check**, and **w_save**, using the equivalent deposit programs as models. This will complete the withdraw module of the ATM. Note: The maximum sum of money that can be withdrawn from the checking account is the present checking balance plus the credit limit. The maximum sum that can be withdrawn from the savings account is the savings balance.

4-8 Complete the **to_check** program, using **to_save** as a model. This will complete the transfer module of the system. Note: The maximum sum that can be transferred from one account to another is the balance of the first account.

4-9 Inspect all the programs you've written thus far, and make sure you've recorded the details of the last transaction according to the rules of the game (page 134). Next, complete the programs **i_check**, **i_save**, and **i_last**, thus completing the information module of the system. Test this module rigorously by running withdrawals, deposits, and transfers, and by displaying the last transaction information after each transaction.

4-10 Use the **CREATE** command to build an **accounts** file for the ATM system. Make sure the file's structure and contents are identical to those displayed on page 133. Next, index the file on the **pin** field.

4-11 Rewrite the **setup** program so that it will fully implement stages 1, 2, and 3.1 in the ATM logic (page 134). (Hints: Open the **accounts** file on the **PIN** index, and **SEEK mpin**. If the search is successful, set **found** to **.T.** and copy the fields of the current record onto variables by using the commands **mcbal=cbal**, and so on. Also, remove the line **PUBLIC mpin, mcbal, msbal, mlim, mlastsum, mlastop, mlastdate** from the **setup** program, and insert instead the line **PRIVATE mpin, mcbal, msbal, mlim, mlastsum, mlastop, mlastdate** at the top of the **atm** program.) Test the program on various customers (including customers who provide bad PIN numbers).

4-12 Rewrite the **update** program so that it will implement fully stage 3.3 in the ATM logic (page 134). (Hint: use the **REPLACE** command.) Test the program on various customers, and make sure the ending balance of one session is the same as the beginning balance of the next session (for the same customer).

4-13 Consider the following suggestion: Since the ATM system handles all the customer's transactions in main memory, there is no need to tie up the **accounts** file throughout the session. A better strategy would be to close the file at the end of the **setup** program (after the customer's record has been retrieved), use variables to process the customer's transactions, and reopen the file for update purposes just before the session's end (i.e., at the beginning of the **update** program). What do you think of this suggestion?

4-14 Modify the ATM system so that it will accommodate an *accounts manager* as well as bank customers. The accounts manager identifies himself or herself by a special PIN number, say 1111. If this PIN number is entered, the system branches to a new module that enables the addition, editing, and deletion of customer accounts, under the control of a menu-driven user interface. Note: This module amounts to a major extension of the present system.

Postscript

It is fitting to conclude this chapter with the following passage, written by D.D. McCracken, with slight modifications:[1]

---

[1] *Encyclopedia of Computer Science and Engineering*, Van Nostrand Reinhold Company, 1983)

Modular Programming: Good system design starts with the most general definition of the function of the system, and proceeds through a sequence of increasingly detailed specifications, all the way down to writing individual programs. This technique is sometimes called "top-down design" or "stepwise refinement."

In the development of a large software system by a team of programmers, good modularization is essential if the portions written by different programmers are to mesh effectively and in a reasonable period of time into a system. Furthermore, since all systems that are used over a period of time have to be maintained and modified, good modularization also aids in doing these chores more quickly and accurately.

A module can be defined as a logically self-contained and discrete part of a larger system. A complete system can thus be considered to be a collection of modules. A properly constructed module accepts input that is well-defined as to content and structure, carries out a well-defined set of processing actions, and produces output that is well-defined as to content and structure.

The purpose of modular programming is to break a complex task into smaller and simpler subtasks, which, among other things, facilitates writing correct programs. A program consisting of modules of properly designed scope (typically a page or two of code at most) is much simpler to design, write, and test than is the same program when it is not so modularized.

If you've managed to complete the entire ATM system on your own, you should take pride in your accomplishment. You took an active role in the design process of a complex, real-life system that can be easily converted into a commercial product. Now, without discounting your own contribution, note that a great deal of credit is due to the system's *modularity.* If the ATM system were not modular, you would not be able to extend it without creating a monster in the process. This modularity was the result of a careful systems analysis effort that preceded the writing of this chapter. Many systems fail because people rush to write programs before they think clearly what it is they want to do. If you have read this book and have done all the exercises, you should know better than that. You can't start a software consulting business yet, but you're getting close.

A Program Development Guide

Programming can be described in terms of the following cycle: make errors, detect errors, diagnose errors, fix errors, and, in the process, make new errors, and so on. This appendix discusses each of these steps in detail. We'll skip the first step, *making errors*, trusting that the reader will master this material on his or her own.

If this is the first time you are reading this appendix, please read it in its entirety, doing all the exercises as you go along. This will give you a complete picture of the program development cycle in dBASE. After the first reading, you can continue to use this appendix for reference.

Design First, Program Later

Writing a computer program is like building a house. You can't start laying bricks without having a clear plan of the underlying structure. Similarly, if you want to write a good program, you must *design* it first. Start by sketching the logical flow of the program on paper, using English, pseudocode, or any language of your choice. When you think you have a good model of the program, proceed to translate it to dBASE. Next, put yourself in the shoes of the interpreter, and try to execute the program on paper, tracking its flow of control and verifying that it produces the desired output.

It's essential to do these activities away from the computer, using paper and pencil only. The most common error of first-time programmers is to try to write programs from scratch, using a text editor. This is a bad strategy because the keyboard has a chilling effect on the ability of humans to think logically. Once your fingers start to do the walking, your mind will focus on how to avoid the next typing error. This state of mind is guaranteed to produce lousy programs.

If, however, you've hand-simulated your program on paper, you should know with confidence that the program is logically correct. Only then should you take your notes to the computer, key in the program, and proceed to test it. This will bring you to the most critical and laborious stage in the program development cycle: debugging. Programming errors are called **bugs**, and the art of exterminating bugs is called **debugging**.

This appendix walks you through the process of creating, editing, testing, debugging, printing, and logging dBASE programs. The programming tools that are presented below make up a simple but effective software development environment designed specifically for the readers of this book.

Getting Help

In addition to the paper-based documentation that comes with dBASE, the system features an elaborate user's guide that is stored right on the disk. You can open this guide at the page of your choice by entering the command **HELP**, followed by the name of a specific command. For example, if you want help about the **INPUT** command, enter **HELP IN-PUT**. After reading the help screen, press **ESC** to go back to interactive mode. For more information about **HELP**, try **HELP HELP**.

Two words of caution: (1) Contrary to what you may expect, the help information is not intended for beginners. Rather, it should be used as a source of reference for people who already know some dBASE. (2) In dBASE IV, the organization of the help screens is somewhat annoying. First, the screens are small and cluttered. Second, it's somewhat difficult to recognize when you are crossing the boundary from one help topic to another. Still, the help screens in both versions of dBASE are quite useful, provided you have a general idea of what you are doing.

Exercise A-1 Use **HELP** to get acquainted with the **DO WHILE** command. You don't have to understand this command fully—just get a general feeling of how it works.

Writing a Program

Recall that a *file* is a designated area on the computer's disk that stores certain information. Depending on its size and density, a single disk can contain several dozen to several thousand files. The contents of each individual file can be anything: a resume, a letter, a poem, a shopping list, or a dBASE program, to mention only a few examples. A **text editor**, or *editor* for short, is a computer program that enables you to create new files and edit existing files. A **word processor** is a fancy editor.

dBASE features a simple text editor that goes by the funny name **MODI COMM**—a shorthand of **MODIFY COMMAND**. As you start using the editor, you'll realize the term **MODIFY COMMAND** is somewhat misleading. First, the editor can be used not only to *modify* files, but also to *create* them from scratch. Second, the editor is not restricted to programs ("command files") only; you can use it to create or edit *any* text file of your choice.

For example, suppose you want to compose a draft of your resume, and you decide to store it in a file that you prudently name **resume.txt** (as opposed to, say, **gnu45.cfg**). When you are ready to begin writing, enter the command **MODI COMM resume.txt** from interactive mode. If a file named **resume.txt** does not exist on the disk, the editor will create an empty one from scratch. If the file exists on the disk, the editor will enable you to change it by deleting, modifying, or adding new text.

Exercise A-2   In this exercise you are asked to write a brief resume that contains your name, career objective, and previous experience with computers (if any). Begin by entering the command **MODI COMM resume.txt**. This will put you "inside" the editor screen. Next, proceed to write a few lines of text, as if you were using a typewriter (to start a new line, press the **ENTER** key). If you make a typing error, use the keys ←, →, ↓, and ↑ to position the cursor on the erroneous text, then press the **DEL** key to erase it.

Please keep your resume short—no longer than ten lines of text. When you have finished writing it, press the two keys **CTRL END** (first press **CTRL**, then press **END** while **CTRL** is still depressed). This will instruct the editor to save your work on the disk and put you back into interactive mode. If you want to inspect the file on the screen, enter the command **TYPE resume.txt**. If you want to correct it, enter **MODI COMM resume.txt**. When you have finished, print the file on paper by using the command **DO lprint**. This utility program will ask you to enter the filename (**resume.txt**) and your own name, and will then proceed to send the file to the printer.

The Editing Process   If you did the last exercise, you probably agree that computer-based editing is quite easy, once you get the basic hang of it. The purpose of this section is to give you an in-depth understanding of what takes place under the surface, so to speak, when you enter the command **MODI COMM**. This knowledge will prove useful when you have to deal with the dark side of editing, such as restoring a file to its original version after you've accidently messed it up in the editor.

As it turns out, the editing process involves not *one*, but *three*, different files: the file you wish to edit, a backup copy, and a memory-resident copy (i.e., a copy of the file stored in the computer's main memory rather than on the disk). The interpreter creates and manages the latter two files automatically, whenever you invoke the editor. The relationship among the three files is important, and an example might help to illustrate it.

Suppose you enter the command **MODI COMM myprog**. The following procedure, written in pseudocode, describes the various steps the interpreter will take to execute this command:

1. Search the disk for a file named **myprog.prg**
2. **IF** there is such a file:
          Create a memory-resident version of the file
   ELSE:
          Initialize a memory-resident version of the file
   ENDIF
3. Let the user edit the memory-resident version of the file
   (this might take a few minutes to a few hours)
4a. **IF** the user wishes to exit the editor and save
       the changes (by pressing the keys **CTRL END**):
       Make a backup copy of **myprog.prg**,
       and call it **myprog.bak**; copy the
       memory-resident version onto **myprog.prg**;
       return to interactive mode
   ENDIF
4b. **IF** the user wishes to exit the editor without
       saving (by pressing the **ESC** key):
       return to interactive mode
   ENDIF

Hence, instead of editing the file **myprog.prg**, which is stored on the computer's *disk*, you'll be actually editing a copy of the file, stored in the computer's *memory*. Therefore, if there is a power failure in the midst of your editing, you will lose all the changes you've made since you last entered the editor, but the original file—**myprog.prg**—will remain intact. This is due to the difference between long-term and short-term storage media: the disk is made of magnetic material, which stores data permanently, whereas main memory represents data through electric charges, which disappear once the computer is turned off.

Exiting the Editor: As specified in stages 4a and 4b of the procedure just shown, there are two ways to exit the editor. If you want to save your changes on the disk, enter **CTRL END**. If you want to exit the editor without saving your changes, enter **ESC**. The latter option is quite handy because editing is not always a step in the right direction. Often you'll regret your recent changes, wishing to leave the original version of the file intact, just as it was before you started to change it. This can be easily accomplished, at any time, by pressing the **ESC** key.

The prg Extension: As a rule, all dBASE program files must have the extension **prg**. Now, since the dBASE editor is used primarily to write programs, the interpreter makes the reasonable assumption that what you are editing is indeed a program. Therefore, if you don't specify a file extension, the interpreter automatically adds the default extension **prg** to your chosen filename. If you *do* specify an extension, as in **MODI COMM resume.txt**, the interpreter will leave the extension as is.

The Backup File: When you instruct the editor to save your changes, the editor assumes you may change your mind later. Instead of simply replacing the original version of **myprog.prg** with the new version, the editor first creates a backup of the original version, naming it **myprog.bak**. This safety measure gives you two layers of security, as follows. If you want to exit the editor without saving your changes, press **ESC**, as we just explained. If you regret your changes *after* you've saved them and exited the editor, you can still restore the original version of the file by entering the interactive command **COPY FILE myprog.bak TO myprog.prg**.[1]

THE dBASE EDITOR

The standard dBASE literature contains a detailed documentation of the dBASE editor, and we won't repeat this material here. In practice, one needs no more than ten percent of the editor's functionality in order to get most jobs done. This ten percent is described in the following table (the starred commands are available only in dBASE IV):

---

[1] On some rare occasions, you might at that point get the error message **file already open**. If this happens, quit dBASE, reenter it, and try the **COPY** command again. This time it will work.

Press:	To:
←	Move the cursor left
→	Move the cursor right
↓	Move the cursor down
↑	Move the cursor up
HOME	Move the cursor to the beginning of the line (★)
END	Move the cursor to the end of the line (★)
CTRL N	Insert a new line at the cursor position
DEL	Delete the character at the cursor position
CTRL Y	Delete the entire line at the cursor position
CTRL END	Save the changes and return to interactive mode
ESC	Return to interactive mode without saving the changes
CTRL ENTER	Save the changes without returning to interactive mode (★)
F1	Display help information (That's an on/off switch)
F10	Display the editing commands menu (★)

If you want to learn more about the dBASE editor (which is not the most fascinating subject in the world), you may either refer to your standard dBASE literature or enter **MODI COMM** and press **F1** for interactive help.

Exercise A-3   Consider the following program, written by the programmer Clyde McBug. The program is supposed to display the word **hello** five times on the screen:

```
x=0
DO WHILE y<5
    ? 'Hello
ENDDO
RETURN
```

Invoke the dBASE editor and create this program, storing it in the file **hello.prg**. In other words, enter the command **MODI COMM hello**, and go on to type the program *exactly* the way it appears here. At this point you should neither understand the program nor notice that it contains some errors.

A Note to dBASE III PLUS Users: If you've installed the book's data disk correctly, the editor will operate in *insert* mode. You may switch to *overwrite* mode (and back to *insert*) by pressing the key marked **INS** on the keyboard. As you start using the editor, though, you'll quickly discover it's much easier to work in *insert* mode.

Displaying a Program

If you want to take a quick look at a certain program, say **myprog**, there is no need to invoke the editor. You can display the program from interactive mode by entering the command **TYPE myprog.prg**. Note that unlike the **MODI COMM** command, you must specify the **prg** extension here. Otherwise, you'll get the error message **file does not exist: myprog**.

Exercise A-4 Display the **hello** program on the screen. Compare it to the program on the previous page, and make sure there are no discrepancies. If there are discrepancies, use the editor to resolve them.

Running a Program

Programs are executed through the **DO** command. To run a program, say **myprog**, enter **DO myprog**. Before you do so, remember that about ninety percent of the programs that are executed for the first time contain errors. The remaining ten percent are so defective that they don't even start running.

Exercise A-5 In addition to the **hello** program, which contains errors, your disk contains an error-free version of the same program, named **hello5**. Run **hello5**, inspect its output, and verify that it's doing what it's supposed to do.

Testing a Program

The dBASE editor is very useful in terms of *writing* a program, but it provides no means to *validate* the contents of the program—that is, to make sure that it conforms to the syntax rules of dBASE. In fact, the editor is not even aware that you are using it to write a dBASE program. As far as the editor is concerned, the text you are entering can be anything—a program, a love letter, a dissertation, whatever.

It is therefore not surprising that most programs contain numerous errors when they are first executed. All you have to do is misspell a command or forget a comma somewhere, and the whole program will come to a screeching halt. you don't need to feel bothered by this, however. Committing and fixing errors is a normal part of the program development process, and there's no way to avoid it.

To see this illustrated, try to rerun the **hello** program. Since the program contains errors, the interpreter will halt its execution, displaying the messages **Variable not found: Y**, and **Unterminated string**. An inspection of the program reveals that both messages make sense. First, the variable in the second line should be **x**, not **y**. We know this because we can see from the program's structure that McBug probably wanted x to "count" how many times the **WHILE** loop would be executed. The second error, which is much easier to figure out, is in the third line: the string **hello** should be followed by a single quotation mark. Please enter the editor, correct both errors, and rerun the program.

Something odd is happening. The program runs all right, but it doesn't seem to stop! In fact, the program will continue to say **hello** until the end of the world, or until you press the **ESC** key—whichever comes first. Let's take a look at the code and try to figure out what is going on.

First, note that **DO WHILE** is not a simple command. If this is the first time you have seen it, here is how it works: The interpreter is instructed to display **hello** lines on the screen as long as **x** is less than 5. After displaying the first **hello**, the interpreter goes back to check the value of **x**. If it's still less than 5, the interpreter displays another **hello**, goes back to check the value of **x**, and so on.

Well, it's no wonder the program never stops. The value of **x** was initialized to 0 at the beginning of the program, and was never changed anywhere else in the program. Therefore, **x** will always be less than 5, and the interpreter would run circles inside the **DO WHILE** loop forever. Thank goodness the program doesn't send its output to the printer!

Exercise A-6 It looks as if McBug wanted **x** to serve as a counter, but he forgot to *increment* it every time he displayed **hello**. To fix the error, we have to do something that will cause **x** to change from 0 to 1, to 2, to 3, to 4, and then to 5, each time we display **hello** on the screen. This can be done by inserting the command **x=x+1** after the command **? 'hello'**.

In this exercise you are required to do three things: (1) use the editor to add this line, (2) test the program to be sure that it produces the desired output, and (3) modify the program so it will display **hello** 12 times instead of 5. When you have finished, step back and try to understand (at least intuitively) the cyclical nature of this program.

Syntax and Run-Time Errors   All programming errors fall into two distinct categories: **syntax** errors, and **run-time** (also called **logical**) errors. Syntax errors occur when you "misspell" a command, say **INPUT x** instead of **INPUT TO x**. Run-time errors occur when a syntactically correct program does something weird. Programs that deal with user-supplied inputs are especially prone to run-time errors. For example, consider the following program, designed to compute the value of the mathematical expression $\frac{x}{x-y}$:

```
INPUT TO x
INPUT TO y
? x/(x-y)
RETURN
```

The program is syntactically correct. Therefore, it might work flawlessly for thousands of times, until—until it gets two equal numbers as inputs. This will cause the program to bomb, since the interpreter can't divide by 0.

Note that syntax errors are relatively easy to handle: the interpreter will find them for you, displaying error messages in the process. The messages may not mean much, but they will at least tell you that *something went wrong*. Run-time errors are much harder to detect, because they occur only with certain inputs. The problem, of course, is that when it comes to a complex and lengthy program, it is simply impossible to test it against all the possible combinations of inputs that it might ever encounter.

Therefore, the common practice is to test the program only against *typical* input patterns. For example, although the user can enter any two numbers, x and y, into the above program, the interesting cases are $x > y$, $x < y$, and $x = y$. Thus, it is sufficient to test the program on, say, the pairs of numbers (5,7), (7,5), and (5,5). This will be much more productive than testing it on, say, (5,7), (213,777), and (11,19).

In summary, it is your responsibility as a programmer to discover which inputs would bring a program to its knees, and then write the necessary code to prevent this from happening (we haven't discussed this part yet). It would be nice if we could design a testing device that could read *any* program and certify whether it will *always* terminate its execution properly. Before you rush to start a new software company, though, be advised that such a device cannot be built, as was proved by the mathematician Alan Turing back in the 1930s. Hence, the best we can do is test the program rigorously and systematically, hoping we have covered most, if not all, its possible input patterns.

The critical role of software testing has given rise to a new profession: testing engineers. A testing engineer specializes in detecting and diagnosing errors in programs that other people have written. The job requires a great deal of programming expertise, as well as plain common sense. In addition, a good testing engineer must exercise pessimism and skepticism (during working hours, that is). The testing engineer must assume that anything that can go wrong, will go wrong, and he or she should never rely on oral or written statements about program behavior. The only way to test a program is to run it and let it speak for itself.

Debugging a Program

dBASE is sometimes sloppy in diagnosing errors. When the interpreter encounters an error, it makes a pathetic effort to explain what happened. If you feel this explanation is off the wall, you're probably right. At that point, you may want to invoke the interactive **HELP** command, refer to this book, or do what all programmers do—use the trial-and-error method. In programming, this means revising the program and rerunning it, hoping the revision has introduced fewer errors than it has eliminated.

As you know by now, the only way to fix a defective program is to load it into the editor, edit the part that is presumably responsible for the error, save the program, exit to interactive mode, and try to **DO** it again. This trial-and-error process will continue until you have sorted out all the errors from the program.

When the interpreter detects an error in a program, it halts its execution with an error message. Depending on the nature of the error, the interpreter will allow you to do one of three things:

CANCEL: This option terminates the program's execution and puts you back into interactive mode. This will enable you to invoke the editor and try to fix the program.

IGNORE: This option instructs the interpreter to ignore the error and execute the remainder of the program. This typically leads to nonsensical program behavior.

SUSPEND: This option instructs the interpreter to withhold the program's execution until further notice. When you type the magic word **RESUME**, the interpreter will continue to execute the program.

The **SUSPEND** option is handy. It freezes the program's execution precisely in the line that caused the error, and puts you back into interactive mode. Since the program is still alive, you can display its variables by using the **?** command. This will give you a good idea about what the program is trying to do. When you are ready to resume the program's execution, enter the command **RESUME**.

The **SUSPEND** command is equally useful in *batch mode.* Savvy programmers place several **SUSPEND** commands in strategic or "weak" points in their code. This enables them to anticipate problems and plan the debugging schedule in advance. When they feel the program is error-free, they remove all the **SUSPEND** commands from the code.

DEBUGGING IN dBASE III PLUS

The style by which the interpreter executes programs can be altered by manipulating three "switches," named **STEP**, **ECHO**, and **TALK**. The details are as follows:

SET STEP ON: This switch setting instructs the interpreter to pause before the execution of any program line, until you press the **ENTER** key. This enables you to step through the program's execution at your own pace, pressing **ENTER** whenever you are ready to execute the next command.

SET ECHO ON: This switch setting causes the interpreter to display on the screen each program line, just after it gets executed.

SET TALK ON: This switch setting causes the interpreter to display on the screen the value of each variable, whenever a command changes the value of this variable.

The basic idea is to slow down the interpreter's execution with the use of different **ON/OFF** combinations of the three switches. Some people enter **SET ECHO ON**, leaving the other switches **OFF**. Other people have different habits. You may want to experiment with different combinations of these switches until you have developed your own debugging style.

When you have finished your debugging, don't forget to **SET** the three switches **OFF**, as they tend to create an incredible clutter on the screen.

If you find the above confusing, here is a simple debugging prescription. When you want to debug a program, say **myprog**, enter **DO debugon**, followed by **DO myprog**. When you wish to quit debugging, enter **DO debugoff**. These two utility programs are part of the book's software, and they are available on your disk.

We end this section with two warnings to dBASE III PLUS users:

Warning 1: One notorious user-error in dBASE III PLUS programming is forgetting to terminate an **IF** with an **ENDIF**, a **CASE** with an **ENDCASE**, or a **DO WHILE** with an **ENDDO**. Unfortunately, the dBASE III PLUS interpreter is not capable of detecting these trivial errors. Instead, it will cheerfully execute your defective program, producing some unexpected output in the process. Hence, when your program behaves strangely, and you can't think of any other explanation, look for missing **ENDIF**, **ENDCASE**, or **ENDDO**. Chances are that this is the cause of your agony.

Warning 2: On some rare occasions, when you try to load a file into the editor, the interpreter displays the error message **file already open**. When this happens, try the command **CLOSE ALL**, and then reenter the editor. If you still get this error message, quit dBASE and reenter it.

DEBUGGING IN dBASE IV

dBASE IV features an interactive debugger. A **debugger** is a program that enables the programmer to trace the program's flow of control, and, furthermore, to intervene in its execution in a number of ways. Note that the debugger will be useful only after you've sorted out all the syntax errors from the program. In other words, the debugger is designed to help deal with run-time errors "only." The last word was put in quotation marks because detecting run-time errors is really where all the action is.

To debug a certain program, say **myprog**, enter the command **DE-BUG myprog**. If the program is free of syntax errors, you will see the debugger's screen, which is divided into five windows. The two most important windows are at the top-left corner, where the program is displayed, and at the bottom-left corner, where one can enter various commands to control the debugger's activity.

The standard literature on dBASE IV contains a good coverage of the debugger, so we won't repeat that material here. As usual, the best way to learn how the debugger works is to use it.

Exercise A-7   Enter the command **DEBUG hello**, and take a look at the screen. Next, press **ENTER** once. This will cause the interpreter to execute the first line of the program, a fact which will be seen quite vividly in the top-left window. Then press **ENTER** again, and watch the interpreter execute the next line in the program. Continue to press **ENTER** until you've executed the command **? 'hello'**. Next, press the **F9** function key. This will display the output that the end-user will see when actually *running* (as opposed to *debugging*) the same program. To go back to the debugger, press **F9** again. Then continue to step through the program by pressing **ENTER**, until the program terminates its execution. (It might be a good idea to press **F9** every once in a while, to keep track of the program's outputs.) For more information about the debugger's capabilities, press **F1** for interactive help, and refer to your standard dBASE literature.

Halting a Program

The execution of any program can be halted at any time by pressing the **ESC** key. This comes in handy when dealing with a program that goes berserk—especially if it uses the printer in the process.

Printing a Program

To print a program (or any other text file) on paper, enter the command **DO lprint**. Next, you'll be asked to enter (1) the program's name and (2) your own name. After you have provided this information, the program will be printed on paper, following a little banner that carries your name and today's date. If you work in a computer lab in which fifty students are simultaneously sending the same program to the same printer, this banner will be the only way to identify your output from the rest of the crowd.

Recording an Interactive Session

There are various reasons why you may want to create a printed transcript of a dBASE session. First, you can incorporate the transcript into a document prepared by a word processor (that's how all the transcripts in this book were created). Second, if you experience a bug you can't handle, you can repeat the actions that led to the bug (for recording purposes), print the transcript, and take it to a consultant. Finally, if you have to show your instructor how your program works, you can hand in a transcript of a session that illustrates its execution.

In dBASE, an interactive session can be recorded under the user's control on a background file called an **ALTERNATE** file. The details are as follows:

Action	Commands
Start a new transcript	SET ALTERNATE TO log.txt
Begin recording	SET ALTERNATE ON
Suspend recording	SET ALTERNATE OFF
Print the transcript	CLOSE ALTERNATE
	DO lprint (with log.txt)

The first command, **SET ALTERNATE TO log.txt**, doesn't record anything. It only *initializes* the alternate file to be **log.txt** (you can use other filenames if you wish). To actually start recording, enter **SET ALTERNATE ON**. From this point on, the recording process is cumulative: as long as you don't instruct anything to the contrary, everything you see on the screen will be recorded on **log.txt**. If, at any stage, you wish to do some wild experiments in interactive mode without having your actions recorded, enter **SET ALTERNATE OFF**. This will suspend recording until further notice. When you want to resume the recording, enter **SET ALTERNATE ON**. To print the transcript, close **log.txt** by entering the command **CLOSE ALTERNATE**, and then use **DO lprint** to send **log.txt** to the printer.

Important Note 1: The command **SET ALTERNATE TO log.txt** is *destructive* in one sense. If there is already a **log.txt** file on the disk, this command will erase its contents and start it afresh.

Important Note 2: The command **CLOSE ALTERNATE** is *terminal* in one sense. Once you've entered it, there is no way to resume the present recording on the file **log.txt**. The only useful thing to do with **log.txt** at that point is to print it out.

With these two notes in mind, you should try to keep your transcripts short. If you are testing two unrelated programs, don't record them in one long transcript. Instead, record the first program, print the transcript, and then start a new transcript for the second program. Note that once you have a good printout of the file **log.txt**, there is no need to retain a copy of it on the disk. Therefore, you will find it helpful to always use the same name for your alternate files (such as **log.txt**). That way, your disk will never get cluttered with useless transcript files.

The only time you will need to use more than one transcript file is when you are recording the session on one computer and printing it on another. If you happen to work in such a setting, you can create several transcript files on the first computer (e.g., **log1.txt, log2.txt**, and so on). Then insert your disk to the second computer and print all of them by successive applications of **DO lprint**.

Putting It All Together

The process of writing, debugging, and submitting a programming assignment involves eleven stages, as follows:

```
1. Design the program on paper
2. Enter the program into the text-editor
3. Test the program on various inputs
4. DO WHILE the program is not good:
              load the program into the editor,
              fix the error(s),
              exit the editor,
              test the program on various inputs
   ENDDO
*  Note: at this stage the program must be good
5. Initialize a new recording
   (SET ALTERNATE TO log.txt)
6. Begin recording
   (SET ALTERNATE ON)
7. Use TYPE to display the program's code
   (for recording purposes)
8. Test the program again
   (for recording purposes)
9. Close the recording
   (CLOSE ALTERNATE)
10. Print the transcript
    (DO lprint with log.txt)
11. Hand-in the transcript to your instructor
12. Complain about the grade
```

The last stage can be avoided if you take the following tips into consideration:

- A program should speak for itself. Don't annotate the program's code with handwritten comments that explain what the program is doing. That kind of documentation should be an integral part of the code (in the form of comments).

- It's O.K. to annotate the *output* of the program with handwritten remarks like "I'm not sure what happened here." These comments will help your instructor give you useful feedback.

■ It's difficult to create an error-free transcript. The transcript is a printed record of an interactive session, and it often contains embarrassing evidence about the struggle of human with computer. The thing to remember is not to worry about aesthetics. Before you hand in the transcript, take a pen and cross out everything you don't want your instructor to read or grade.

■ Some programming assignments explicitly specify on which inputs the program ought to be tested. For example, you may be asked to write a program that inputs a number and computes its square root, and test it on the numbers 16, −5, and 0. As long as you develop the program, it's O.K. to test it on other inputs as well. However, the transcript you hand in should include tests on no more, and no less, than the numbers 16, −5, and 0.

  If a certain input causes the program to bomb, don't conceal this fact; instead, put it on the record. On the other hand, you should also avoid redundant testing. Just show how the program works on the *inputs you were asked to test it on.*

■ A programming assignment is not an all-or-nothing affair. If you can't get a program right, it's not the end of the world. Hand in a partial transcript that shows the code of your incomplete program and whatever execution you've managed to squeeze out of it.

Index

About the Author

Shimon Schocken is Assistant Professor of Information Systems at New York University's Leonard N. Stern School of Business. He holds a B.A. from the Hebrew University of Jerusalem, an M.B.A. from Indiana University, and a Ph.D. from the Wharton School at the University of Pennsylvania. His doctoral thesis on uncertainty management in expert systems won the 1987 ICIT award for the best information systems dissertation written in the U.S.A., Europe, and Canada. His research and teaching interests are decision theory in artificial intelligence, modeling, and computer literacy.